Maltese in Michigan

DISCOVERING THE PEOPLES OF MICHIGAN

Arthur W. Helweg, Russell M. Magnaghi, and Linwood H. Cousins, *Series Editors*

Ethnicity in Michigan: Issues and People
Jack Glazier and Arthur W. Helweg

African Americans in Michigan
Lewis Walker, Benjamin C. Wilson,
and Linwood H. Cousins

Albanians in Michigan
Frances Trix

Amish in Michigan
Gertrude Enders Huntington

Arab Americans in Michigan
Rosina J. Hassoun

Asian Indians in Michigan
Arthur W. Helweg

Belgians in Michigan
Bernard A. Cook

Chaldeans in Michigan
Mary C. Sengstock

Copts in Michigan
Eliot Dickinson

Cornish in Michigan
Russell M. Magnaghi

Dutch in Michigan
Larry ten Harmsel

Finns in Michigan
Gary Kaunonen

French Canadians in Michigan
John P. DuLong

Germans in Michigan
Jeremy W. Kilar

Greeks in Michigan
Stavros K. Frangos

Hungarians in Michigan
Éva V. Huseby-Darvas

Irish in Michigan
Seamus P. Metress and Eileen K. Metress

Italians in Michigan
Russell M. Magnaghi

Jews in Michigan
Judith Levin Cantor

Latinos in Michigan
David A. Badillo

Latvians in Michigan
Silvija D. Meija

Lithuanians in Michigan
Marius K. Grazulis

Mexicans and Mexican Americans in Michigan
Rudolph Valier Alvarado
and Sonya Yvette Alvarado

Norwegians in Michigan
Clifford Davidson

Poles in Michigan
Dennis Badaczewski

Scandinavians in Michigan
Jeffrey W. Hancks

Scots in Michigan
Alan T. Forrester

South Slavs in Michigan
Daniel Cetinich

Yankees in Michigan
Brian C. Wilson

Discovering the Peoples of Michigan is a series of publications examining the state's rich multicultural heritage. The series makes available an interesting, affordable, and varied collection of books that enables students and educated lay readers to explore Michigan's ethnic dynamics. A knowledge of the state's rapidly changing multicultural history has far-reaching implications for human relations, education, public policy, and planning. We believe that Discovering the Peoples of Michigan will enhance understanding of the unique contributions that diverse and often unrecognized communities have made to Michigan's history and culture.

Maltese in Michigan

Joseph M. Lubig

Michigan State University Press

East Lansing

☉ The paper used in this publication meets the minimum requirements
of ANSI/NISO Z39.48-1992 (R 1997) (Permanence of Paper).

Michigan State University Press
East Lansing, Michigan 48823-5245

Printed and bound in the United States of America.

18   17   16   15   14   13   12   11   1   2   3   4   5   6   7   8   9   10

LIBRARY OF CONGRESS CATALOGING-IN-PUBLICATION DATA
Lubig, Joseph M.
Maltese in Michigan / Joseph M. Lubig.
p. cm. — (Discovering the peoples of Michigan)
Includes bibliographical references and index.
ISBN 978-1-61186-019-1 (paper : alk. paper) 1. Maltese Americans—Michigan—History.
2. Maltese Americans—Michigan—Social life and customs. 3. Maltese Americans—Michigan—
Ethnic identity. 4. Immigrants—Michigan—History. 5. Michigan—Ethnic relations. 6. Michigan—
Social life and customs. 7. Michigan—Emigration and immigration—History. 8. Malta—
Emigration and immigration—History. I. Title.
F575.M34L83 2011
305.892'790774—dc22
2011006449

Cover design by Ariana Grabec-Dingman
Book design by Charlie Sharp, Sharp Des!gns, Lansing, Michigan

Cover photo: Maltese girls pose for a group photo prior to the performance of their play.
Photo courtesy of the Zampa Family.

Michigan State University Press is a member of the Green Press Initiative and
is committed to developing and encouraging ecologically responsible publishing practices. For more information about the Green Press Initiative and the use
of recycled paper in book publishing, please visit *www.greenpressinitiative.org.*

Visit Michigan State University Press on the World Wide Web at *www.msupress.msu.edu*

SERIES ACKNOWLEDGMENTS

Discovering the Peoples of Michigan is a series of publications that resulted from the cooperation and effort of many individuals. The people recognized here are not a complete representation, for the list of contributors is too numerous to mention. However, credit must be given to Jeffrey Bonevich, who worked tirelessly with me on contacting people as well as researching and organizing material.

The initial idea for this project came from Mary Erwin, but I must thank Fred Bohm, director emeritus of the Michigan State University Press, for seeing the need for this project, for giving it his strong support, and for making publication possible. Also, the tireless efforts of Keith Widder and Elizabeth Demers, senior editors at Michigan State University Press, were vital in bringing the series to fruition.

Otto Feinstein and Germaine Strobel of the Michigan Ethnic Heritage Studies Center patiently and willingly provided contributor names and gave this project their tireless support. Yvonne Lockwood of the Michigan State University Museum has also suggested and advised contributors.

Many of the maps in the series were prepared by Gregory Anderson at the Geographical Information Systems (GIS) at Western Michigan University under the directorship of David Dickason. Additional maps were contributed by Ellen White.

Other authors and organizations provided comments on various aspects of the work. There are many people that were interviewed by the various authors who will remain anonymous. However, they have enabled the story of their group to be told. The names of many of these contributors are not available, but we are grateful for their cooperation.

Most of all, this work is a tribute to the writers who patiently gave their time to write and share their research findings. Their contributions are noted and appreciated. To them goes most of the gratitude.

ARTHUR W. HELWEG, *Series Co-editor*

Contents

A Short History of Malta

Geography

Homer called Malta the "navel of the sea." This island nation is comprised of five islands lying at midpoint between Europe and Africa off the southern shore of Sicily. Of the five, Malta, Gozo, and Comino (Kemmuna) comprise the area inhabited by the Maltese. It is one of the most densely populated countries. The island group covers approximately 316 square kilometers, equivalent to twice the size of Washington, D.C. Malta's location and natural harbors have made it a sought-after strategic location from the time of the Ottoman Empire through modern day. The name Malta itself is said to come from a Phoenician word meaning "shelter."

Malta is located approximately sixty miles from Sicily. The country is seventeen miles long and nine miles wide. The country boasts no rivers or lakes. The lack of water features combined with the rocky conditions of the island makes agricultural endeavors a bit difficult, but crops of barley, wheat, grapes, potatoes, and cut flowers can be found growing on the islands.

As a result of the country's small size, the population density is high, making it one of the top ten countries in the world in this category and the highest in the European Union, with just under 1,300 people per square kilometer.

Malta currently produces about 20 percent of its food needs and has a limited supply of fresh water. It currently obtains half of its fresh water from

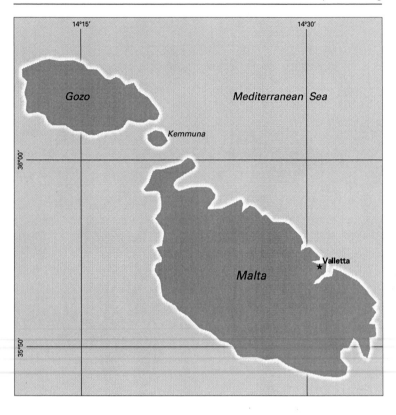

desalination plants. The economy is dependent upon foreign trade, and Malta boasts tourism as its number one financial resource.[1] The geography of the island itself helped it to serve as the location for the 1980 film *Popeye*, starring Robin Williams. The movie was filmed on a set built in Anchor Bay, Mellieha, on the island of Malta. The movie built upon the famous spinach-eating cartoon character and was Robin Williams's movie debut. The island set has since become the site of the Popeye Village Fun Park, where tourists can take in live shows and participate in many land and water activities.[2]

History

Perhaps the history of Malta itself had some doing in preparing those who emigrated from the island to assimilate to the various cultures to which they

St. Paul

St. Paul is the patron saint of Malta. His shipwreck on the northern part of the island in 60 A.D. is described in the Acts of the Apostles. He is credited with converting the Maltese to Christianity during the months he remained on the island, although there is no real historical evidence to support the claim.

While on the island St. Paul is said to have performed several miracles, one of which was to cure the father of the Roman governor, Plubius. Plubius himself went on to become a saint and was ordained as the first bishop of Malta. During his three-month stay St. Paul was also said to have been bitten by a snake. Surviving this bite added to his stature with the natives of the island.

After three months on the island of Malta, St. Paul set sail for Rome, where he would eventually be judged by Caesar and martyred. There is a church dedicated to St. Paul in Mdina. His feast day is celebrated in conjunction with that of St. Peter on June 29.

migrated. The Maltese islands have been conquered repeatedly by empires that have imposed their cultural traditions on the Maltese. Originally settled over 8,000 years ago by an unknown group, the islands have been successively occupied and controlled. The strategic location of Malta and its deep sea port in the middle of the Mediterranean Sea between Italy and Libya made Malta an area of needed control by such powers as the Phoenicians, the Carthaginians, the Romans, the North African Arabs, the Sicilians, various powers in the Middle Ages, the Knights of St. John, the French under Napoleon, and finally the British Empire.[3] Ethnic assimilation became a necessary means of survival, and the history of the islands seems to have been rehearsal for emigration to other countries.

It is a known fact that Malta was inhabited during the Stone Age. The temples on Malta are older than the Egyptian pyramids, dating back over 5,000 years. British archaeologist Colin Renfrew states that "according to the radiocarbon chronology, the temples are the earliest free-standing monuments of stone in the world."[4] Renfrew believes the temples were built around 3000 B.C. As a point of reference, the Great Pyramid in Egypt is dated between 2600 and 2400 B.C.

The Maltese Falcon

Perhaps the most famous cultural reference to Malta is the John Huston film *The Maltese Falcon*. Humphrey Bogart's character is duped into believing that the payment of one falcon per year to King Charles V of Spain was a golden jewel-encrusted falcon worth a fortune. The Maltese Falcon itself served as an excellent plot device for the movie itself.

The Maltese Falcon was nominated for preservation in the United States National Film Registry by the Library of Congress in 1989 as being "culturally, historically, or aesthetically significant." It was accepted into the registry in the first year of voting.

Malta was once under the control of the Phoenicians and the Romans but might be best remembered during this time period for the shipwreck of Saint Paul in A.D. 60, as described in the Acts of the Apostles 27 and 28.

After the fall of the Roman Empire, Malta fell under Byzantine rule until it was occupied by the Arabs in 870. The Arabs brought with them new farming and irrigation techniques that allowed the growth of citrus and cotton on the island. The Arabs also introduced the construction of small rubble walls to stave off erosion of the soil.[5]

During the span of the eleventh to the fourteenth centuries Malta changed hands continually. Rulers during this period include Count Roger the Norman and Roger II, with Malta actually becoming part of the Spanish Empire in 1479, in which it was run as a feudal state.[6]

Malta provided a backstop for Turkish invasion of Rome. The strategic location of Malta helped Charles V and Rome to keep Europe Catholic. Fearing his overthrow, Charles V put Malta in the hands of the Knights of St. John, who were expelled from Rhodes by the Turks in 1522.[7] The payment for Malta to Charles V, Holy Roman Emperor and king of Spain, was one falcon due each year on All Saints' Day.[8]

To be a knight one had to be of noble birth. The Knights of Malta ruled in the spirit of this nobility for more than 250 years until Napoleon took Malta away from them and many of its treasures.[9] While in control of the island the Knights of Malta built an island fortress that withstood the assault of 30,000

Maltese Cross

The Maltese Cross is the symbol of Malta most familiar to non-Maltese. Americans can see its image in the Badge of the Firefighter. The Knights of St. John of Jerusalem gave Malta the heritage of the eight-pointed cross. Growing up I was told that the eight points of the cross represented the eight Beatitudes. Those who have expertise in symbols and the history of their meanings argue that the eight points of the cross represent the eight obligations of a knight.

In 1113 Pope Pascal II recognized the Knights of St. John as the Hospitallers of St. John of Jerusalem, a religious order that bound them to the Augustinian rules of chastity, poverty, and obedience. In addition to these rules, the Hospitallers were required to abide by eight obligations: live in truth, have faith, repent of sin, give proof of humility, love justice, be merciful, be sincere, and endure persecution.

The symbol and meaning of the Maltese Cross has become a badge of honor for the firefighters who work so valiantly to protect human life and property. The New York City Fire Department declares a "firefighter who wears this cross is willing to lay down his life for you just as the crusaders sacrificed their lives for their fellow man so many years ago."

soldiers under the control of the Ottoman Süleyman the Magnificent.[10] When the knights were not at war, they were actively building the city of Valletta in the likeness of the great cities of the world.

After Napoleon's brief period of control, the Maltese petitioned to come under British sovereignty. In 1814 Malta officially became recognized under British rule and maintained this status until after World War II. During the war Malta asserted itself once again as a strategic asset, serving as the military and naval stronghold for the British. The number of bombings from the Axis powers that occurred on Malta during the war was second only to those on Corregidor in the Philippines. President Roosevelt called Malta the "one tiny bright flame in the darkness." King George VI awarded the people of Malta the King George Cross on April 15, 1942, declaring: "To honour her brave people I award the George Cross to the Island Fortress of Malta, to bear witness to a heroism and a devotion that will long be famous in history." The Maltese were the first group in the British Commonwealth to receive this award, usually reserved for individuals, for their bravery during the bombardments.

In response to its loyalty to the Allies during the war, Britain recognized Malta's right to self-govern within the framework of the British Commonwealth in 1947. Malta was recognized as independent from Britain in 1964, with Queen Elizabeth II declared as Queen of Malta.[11] It wasn't until 1974 that Malta became a full republic with the last British troops leaving on March 31, 1979.[12] Malta has been a member of the European Union since 1994.

Perhaps because of its ongoing need to survive the many ruling groups occupying the islands, the Maltese seemed able to overcome barriers existing for other groups coming to the United States: religion, language, and infrequent intermarriage between native populations. Ethnic assimilation and social mobility were already considered desirable by many Maltese prior to moving beyond the borders of their own country.

The Maltese as Early Patriots in America

Maltese in the Colonial Americas

Given the strategic location of Malta in the Mediterranean and the fact that it was tiny and overcrowded, it was natural that Maltese went with the Knights of Malta and other nations to find a new life and opportunity in the Americas. The first governor of New France, Chevalier de Montmagny (1636–1648) was a Knight of Malta and brought associate knights with him. It was at this time that a small Maltese population began to reside in Quebec. Under Montmagny, the Knights provided financial assistance to the first Jesuit missions to the Native Americans.

Between 1651 and 1665 the Knights of Malta developed a small colonial enterprise consisting of a number of islands in the Caribbean. Their outspoken leader, French governor Phillipe de Longvilliers de Poincy, challenged the authority of King Louis XIV and extended their holdings. With the death of Poincy the Knights sold their colonial "empire" to the French West Indies Company. It is possible that during these years Maltese settlers moved to the Caribbean.

In the early eighteenth century, a number of Maltese artillerymen were in rugged Baja California. During a Native American uprising, they distinguished themselves defending the Jesuit missionaries. Viceroy Antonio-Maria de Bucareli (1771–1779) was a Knight of Malta who helped establish

Military Leadership in the Twentieth Century

During Operation Desert Storm, a campaign during the Persian Gulf War of 1991, Brigadier General Patrick P. Caruana commanded the fifty B-52 bombers flying out of Saudi Arabia, England, Spain, and the Indian Ocean.

General Caruana, a St. Louis resident, was also a KC-135 pilot in Vietnam and commanded the Seventeenth Air Division and its fleet of bombers refueling tankers and spy planes.

Alta California and founded some hospitals in Mexico City in the tradition of the Knights of Malta.

The Knights of Malta trained French nobles who entered the French navy during the prerevolutionary era. As a result, when the French navy came to the assistance of the thirteen colonies fighting for their independence against Great Britain, many of the officers were Knights of Malta, and there were Maltese serving aboard the ships.

Unfortunately, few records are available to tell the complete Maltese story in the colonial Americas, but it is obvious that given their history, location, and island environment, it would be natural for some of the Maltese to emigrate to the Americas during these years.

American Revolutionary War

The U.S. embassy's Malta webpage boasts the name of John Pass, a Maltese immigrant, who, along with John Stow, cast the Liberty Bell along with its inscription, "*Proclaim LIBERTY throughout all the Land unto all the Inhabitants thereof Lev. XXV X.*"[13]

The Liberty Bell was made in England in 1751 for the Assembly of the Province of Pennsylvania, to be used in the State House of the City of Philadelphia. Diane Andreassi writes that although "Pass is not a Maltese surname, there is no doubt about his heritage: the speaker of the Pennsylvania Assembly referred to him as hailing from Malta. It is likely that his name in Malta was Pace, and he either changed it, or it was misspelled in documents."[14]

A 1990 article in the *Maltese International*[15] recapped a ceremony

Documented Maltese Immigration during the 1800s

YEAR	MEN	WOMEN	TOTAL
1825			1
1833	3	2	5
1836	2		2
1838			28
1841	42	24	66
1842	1		1
1843	4	1	5
1844	2		2
1846	4		4
1854	2		2
TOTAL			116

Source: William J. Bromwell, *History of Immigration to the United States* (New York: Redfield, 1856).

commemorating Malta's Twenty-fifth Independence Anniversary. This visit occurred during the December 1989 United States / Soviet Union Malta Summit. Here is a segment of the speech given by J. N. Tabone, president of the Maltese Chamber of Commerce:

> Malta's links to the United States of America go back practically to the days of your Founding Fathers.
>
> In fact a Maltese craftsman, John Pace, featured in the saga of American Independence, his name being linked with the Liberty Bell that proclaimed American Independence from the Philadelphia State House in 1776.
>
> During the American revolutionary war, Malta was ruled by the Order of St. John of Jerusalem, the famous Knights of Malta. At that time the order opted for neutrality, but it is known that no less than 1,800 Maltese seamen went to Toulon in France to enlist in the French navy, contributing to the manpower of the French Squadron that was sent to help the American uprising.
>
> The first known diplomatic exchange between Malta and the United States goes back to 1783 when Benjamin Franklin, American Ambassador to

France, struck a special medal to commemorate American Independence. He sent a specimen to Grand Master Emanuel de Rohan who ruled Malta as "a homage of gratitude" and requested Grand Master's protection "for such our citizens as circumstances may lead to your ports."[16]

In addition to the contributions of John Pass (Pace), another Maltese was serving the revolution at sea. Joseph Borg is said to have gone to the aid of the Americans at the time of the American Revolution as a sea captain who fought in many battles for American independence.[17]

Coming to America Prior to World War II

Perhaps the social restrictions placed on males due to the dense population of the country combined with the desire for better paying or more consistent work led to the start of the waves of emigration. The first movement out of the country began in 1883, when seventy workers emigrated from Malta to Queensland, Australia. Political complications put this plan and additional ideas of mass emigration to Australia on hold. At the turn of the nineteenth century Maltese migrants were looking at North Africa, with a few making the journey to Australia and the United States, specifically to New Orleans.[18] As early as 1896 there are records of a Maltese in the U.S. Navy fighting in the Spanish-American War who went back to Malta in 1906, returning in the following year to America, most likely because of a significant downturn in construction on the islands.[19]

The early 1920s began the massive immigration of the Maltese to the Detroit area. As an interview with Marion Zampa about her "papa" and "mama" reflects, the Maltese came to the United States to better their own living conditions and those of their children.

Michael Zampa was the oldest of seven children. He was named after his paternal grandfather. His parents were shopkeepers. They worked hard, as did many of the Maltese people to raise their children. Carmela [Michael's mother] was a good cook, and she enjoyed giving her grandchildren treats when they visited. Being the oldest, Mike had a keen sense of responsibility to help his parents in any way possible. He had a carefree and caring personality. He played as hard as he worked, and several stories that he shared with us related many adventurous outings that he would enjoy with his friends and siblings. His sister Juiette died in 1938, leaving a husband and two children behind. Mike and his family helped with the care of the children, but his sister Pawla took most of the responsibility raising them.

Even though Malta was not directly involved in World War I the economy was affected because of the European financial pressures at the time. It would have been around this time period that Mike, at the age of fifteen, was trying to find a way to leave Malta to be able to earn money for his family. He told stories of how his dad worked hard to earn enough money to feed and care for his children. Mike decided to stow away on a merchant ship leaving Malta for America. He hid on the ship with another boy, hoping not to get caught. The crew found them and took them to their dads. He never gave up trying to get to America. He figured that once in the States he could get a job and send money back home to his family. The next attempt to enter the States was successful.

In April 1920, at the age of sixteen, he obtained passage to America with two men from India. They wanted to start a fabric store in New York. They asked Mike if he wanted a job with them, and he got his dad's permission to go and work for them in New York City. When they got to Ellis Island, U.S. Immigration let Mike enter the States, but they sent the two men back to India. He was alone in New York with very little money and no place to stay. He was able to get a job as a bellhop in a hotel, where they gave him a salary and a place to stay. He wanted to be able to send money home to his parents but wasn't making enough for him to live on. He would walk along the streets of New York looking for ways to earn more money, and came across a sign for the United States Marines. When he went in to join up he didn't weigh very much, so they told him to gain some weight and then come back. He returned after gaining a little more weight. The marines recruiter told him he needed his parents' signatures, but Mike told the recruiter he was in the States by himself and lived on his own. On December 15, 1920, at the age of seventeen, he enlisted in the Marine Corps for two years of duty. He was sent to Quantico, Virginia, for boot camp, then to

ABOVE: Mike Zampa (*middle*) and two unidentified military buddies pose for a photo in Cuba while stationed there with the U. S. Marines. Photo courtesy of the Zampa Family.

RIGHT: Cousins Eddy Camilleri, Mike Zampa, and Paul Camilleri kept strong family ties in the United States, 1920s.

Mike Zampa, serving in the British Navy, Army and Air Force Institutes, at the rail of the HMS *Winchelsea*. Photo courtesy of the Zampa Family.

Cuba. He was stationed there until his tour of duty was over. On December 9, 1922, at the age of nineteen, he was honorably discharged.

During the time after his discharge he worked for the Ford Motor Company. Mike's cousins, Eddy and Paul Camilleri, had immigrated to the States. They both had jobs in Detroit. Paul was an accomplished chef. Mike stayed with them and then returned to Malta a few years later with the hope and dream of returning to the States after a short visit with his family. While in Malta he helped his parents out in their store and enjoyed Malta's social life. Mike and his brother Manuel were very close and did lots of things together. One day the two brothers noticed Stella Bugeja and her sister Netta walking across the street. They introduced themselves, and their romantic history was about to begin. Courtships in Malta are conducted with chaperones, so Netta usually went along whenever Mike wanted to take Stella out. Manuel told Mike that if he didn't propose to Stella, then he would. Mike was in love with Stella and asked for her hand in marriage. He still wanted to return to the States, and on July 16, 1926, he was issued a one-year visitor's visa. Manuel and their friend, Joe Melidon, joined him on this trip to the States. They enjoyed time with Eddy and Paul [Camilleri] and were able to find odd jobs at hotels and restaurants. Mike and Manuel returned to Malta on July 16, 1927. Mike stayed in Malta and worked at his parents' store, married Stella in 1929, and in 1930 joined the Navy, Army, and Air Force Institute (NAAFI) which provided services to the British military. He was assigned to the Royal Navy, serving aboard several destroyers as canteen manager because of his experience and job history as a shopkeeper.

Mike and Stella got married on January 12, 1929, at St. Dominic's Parish, Valletta. This was the parish Stella's family belonged to. Mike's family belonged to St. Paul's in Valletta. Families identified with their parish, and this would be cause for some arguments regarding which one was the best in all their festa celebrations. They had their wedding reception in Sliema. Netta was their bridesmaid and Joseph and Vincent Camilleri were their witnesses. The women in the wedding party are not recorded as witnesses on the official documents. Stella and Mike went to live near her mother in Valletta.[20]

Stories of America brought back to the island of Malta by stowaways[21] combined with government support through the "assisted passage grant" caused emigration to the United States to increase greatly after World War I. Although San Francisco and New York were sites of notable Maltese immigration, Detroit, with its need for cheap and unskilled physical labor, was the city of choice, with a significant population settling in the area of Michigan Avenue and Fifth Street. The predominance of Maltese working as mechanics, electricians, machine operators, and in other trades related to the port cities in which they lived prepared them well to fill the void needed in the Motor City.

One estimate puts the number of Maltese people around Highland Park and Detroit at about 5,000 between 1910 and 1920. Official census figures were not accurate then, as often the Maltese, who had British passports, were counted with the British. Also, because so many entered America illegally, through the back door, so to speak, by jumping ships or crossing the Canadian border at night, they were never counted by the official census takers. However, it is a known fact that the Detroit Maltese group

Mike Zampa (*standing, center*) and unidentified friends gather in Detroit, circa 1920. Photo courtesy of the Zampa Family.

outnumbered their compatriots in New York or California, and continue to do so to this day.[22]

The need to stay connected to the Maltese culture and to begin the assimilation process fostered the development of many Maltese social clubs. This would allow Maltese in Detroit to find friends and family from the old country in a safe and supportive environment.

Tony Agius is said to have attempted to organize the first Maltese social club on Michigan Avenue prior to 1920. This attempt most likely motivated others who saw a continued need for the Maltese to stay connected for social, political, and economic reasons. The Sons of Malta was formed around 1922 as the first sustained group for the Maltese. The Sons of Malta was presided over by John B. Spitery, who was influential in Detroit banking circles until his death in 1961. Records indicate that the main purpose of this club was to promote and support a Maltese soccer team participating in the Detroit American Soccer League.[23]

As with most other ethnic groups, the first club spawned others. The late 1920s saw the Maltese Social Club, led by Joseph Fasi, located on the corner of Trumball Avenue and Forter Street; in 1928 the Ramblers were organized and headquartered at Fifth Street near Elizabeth; and in 1930 the St. Mary's Club formed and resided on Trumbull Avenue.[24]

The clubs, excluding the Maltese Social Club, all hosted skilled soccer teams comprised of Maltese. The exception to a purely Maltese team was the Ramblers, who had to recruit members from the Scottish, Swedish, and English communities to field enough members for a full team. Their recruitment paid off, as the Ramblers became champions of the B Division and A Division semifinalists of the Detroit American Soccer League in 1934.[25]

The *Detroit Free Press* would recognize the Maltese settling in the area as "busy women and earnest men; good sober people looking for work . . . expecting as soon as possible to become American citizens, and to take up our way of life. It is hoped that they will not be forced back to their overcrowded homeland for lack of employment here. They have come so far, they are so eager and willing."[26] Interviews with Maltese reflect this work ethic and willingness to invest in their new community, as evidenced by a desire to own homes. After all, *Id-dar m'hemmx ahjar minnha*: There is nothing better than one's own house.

World War II and Immigration

The Maltese did not come to the America because of political or religious persecution, disease, or famine. The Maltese came to the United States to capture a better life for themselves and for their children. Emigration has been a release valve for the Maltese government, as evidenced by the incentives offered to potential migrants. One of the incentives offered after World War II was the "assisted passage grant," allowing government-sponsored passage for Maltese to emigrate to Canada, England, Australia, and the United States for a fee of $25 (in U.S. money), with the Maltese government paying the rest of the passage. Maltese who agreed to the terms of this "contract" were obligated to stay in their new country for a period of two years. Returning to Malta, and thus violating the agreement, required the emigrant to repay the government for the amount of the passage. As a result of this program, emigration from the islands soared; 11,447 left in 1954 alone. Under this program approximately 8,000 Maltese came to the United States between 1947 and 1977.[27] This put the number of Maltese in Detroit in 1980 at an estimated 44,000.[28]

The second wave of immigration to the United States immediately following World War II brought approximately 6,000 Maltese to America between 1946 and 1955 with the years between 1950 and 1955 representing the peak of migration.[29] In fact, 1950 was a record year when, for the first time, the

Stella and Mike Zampa pose for a photo in Malta just prior
to their departure for the United States of America, 1946.
Photo courtesy of the Zampa Family.

number of migrants was greater than the number of children born.[30] Due
to more stringent immigration policies imposed by the U.S. government
in 1953, the number of immigrants from Malta and other countries began
to decline. For most Maltese, the route to America was regulated by their
membership in the British Commonwealth, which allowed free movement
among member countries and states. Some Maltese first traveled to England,
which allowed for an easy transition to Canada, where many waited for years
to enter the United States because of quota restrictions.[31]

While the majority of Maltese immigrating to Detroit settled in the area
known as Corktown, they began to disperse after 1950, moving to other parts
of Detroit or leaving the city altogether and heading for the newly developing

Doris (last name unknown) enjoys a day at the beach
with Mike and Stella Zampa during their first visit back to
Malta after moving to Detroit, 1955. Photo courtesy of the
Zampa Family.

suburbs to seek employment at one of the Big Three auto companies. "By the
mid-1940's, Detroit had changed from a genteel middle-class turn-of-the-
century town to a massive industrial working-class city due to the phenom-
enal expansion of the auto industry."[32] In order to operate the factory lines
due to this expansion, companies offered wages sufficient enough to draw
many migrants to the Detroit area.[33]

The majority of Maltese arriving in Detroit in the 1940s and 1950s came
as members of family groups. By this time, two generations were represented, that is, parents and children. Maltese was spoken in the home, and
the fathers spoke the English necessary to obtain and retain employment,

Hank, Mike, Margaret, and Stella Zampa landscape the front yard of their new home on Harlow Street in Detroit. Photo courtesy of the Zampa Family.

while the mothers spoke English with varying degrees of proficiency.[34] As was necessary throughout the history of Malta itself, the children became bilingual through the schools, if not at home. Judith M. Calleja recalls a story told by a father who offered a prize soon after arrival to Detroit to the first child who learned one English word that he or she could accurately translate to Maltese. The prize for completing this task was a bicycle.[35] Being bilingual was not limited to the children of the Maltese in the schools. Irene (Zampa) Lubig tells of a time where she aimed to help one of her classmates in English voice his opinion of a teacher he didn't care for: "I told him to call the teacher a 'chooch.' Well, he did and the teacher surprised me by telling me he knew what that meant. So, needless to say, I was a little embarrassed."[36]

As the younger generations of Maltese came of age to marry in the 1960s and 1970s, an overwhelming number of men married Americans, although unmarried women were available in Malta. Perhaps this attitude represented a consciousness reflected in the cultural history of Malta itself, where it was necessary to break down barriers to assimilate with the various conquering cultures. In one case encountered by Calleja[37] a young man returned to Malta to seek a bride, receiving a negative reaction from his peers. They stated that

Irene Zampa (age 3) poses for
one of the last portraits she
will have taken in Malta before
immigrating to the United States.
Photo courtesy of the Zampa
Family.

his choice to return to Malta to obtain a bride would hinder his ability to
become a true American. Most Maltese speak with pride of their origin, and
large numbers of Maltese have returned to visit Malta at least once since
their arrival in Detroit. Many men marrying Americans took their wives on
a trip to Malta shortly after the wedding. Through this promotion of ethnic
intermarriage, Maltese as a spoken language has been rapidly disappearing
since the 1960s, and the children of these marriages speak English almost
exclusively. Among these newer generations, Maltese words and phrases are
spoken only as a novelty to delight grandparents.

The third-generation Maltese in Detroit are mostly the result of interethnic
marriages. Although members of this generation are aware of their Maltese
ancestry, they speak little Maltese and know less of the history of Malta and
are thoroughly American.

The experiences of Angela Farrugia and Mary Sultana after World War
II support the idea of an improved life for close-knit Maltese families in the
United States, in this case in New York City:

We were born and raised in Malta. Our father was in the merchant navy and he would come back from his travels with clothes and stories from all over the world. This made me and my sister curious about life off the island. We would read the Italian magazines about the American movie stars. My parents came over to the United States to work because we wanted them to, as there were not enough jobs for everybody on Malta, and we thought that in the United States everyone lives like kings and queens. We wanted to live here too, but we had to wait until they had an apartment. They have now retired and have gone back to Malta, but I do not think I will ever go back there to live. My children are American.

Malta is nice but there are no jobs and it is boring. It is a small place, you look out your windows and don't see anyone on the street. It is fifty miles out in the Mediterranean, about the size of Bermuda. You never forget you are on an island.

In America I feel like I have more opportunities to do different things. You can make any kind of life for yourself that you want. We have to work very, very hard here; however, we can save to buy a house and make a nice life for ourselves. Life is hard wherever you go. In this world, you have to work to live, and here in this country there is more work. My work is exciting in a printing plant that makes bonds. I like meeting the people who work here, they come from all over the country, and I enjoy meeting so many different kinds of people. I never feel lonely because there is always someone to talk to.

Maltese families are very close. On that small island you can never get away from one another. Here I like seeing all the people on the street who are strangers because there are very few strangers in Malta. I like the privacy that I have here in this country. I feel like I have more opportunities to choose any life that I want here in the United States. I have more freedom to have my own mind. Even though Manhattan is an island, I miss the water. It is not so easy to get to the beach. It is amazing how time changes you. Sometimes I surprise myself how I can adapt and change and go on. My life is very different here but I am used to it and I do not look back—I always hope for something good, but we never know.[38]

One Family's Journey

Through written histories and personal interviews with the seven Zampa children we can see that the path from Malta to America did not always go according to plan. The plans for their journey would be completed in two phases with Michael, the father, traveling to Detroit first with daughters Rosemarie and Yvonne. Stella would stay in Malta with Victor, Henry, Margaret, Marion, and Irene.

Michael Zampa was able to book a flight for him, Yvonne, and Rosemarie aboard a plane to Tunis. The three left on October 6, 1946, aboard a small plane with twelve other passengers. By the time they landed in Tunis only one engine was working on the plane. They would be stranded for seven weeks. Yvonne recalls the adventure of dining in a French restaurant for her birthday and visiting the home of a rich Arab. Rosemarie's account is not so romantic: "Tunis scared the hell out of me. We used to see the women begging in the street and sitting on the ground. When we tried to go to some people's house I remember being chased by a gang of men with knives."[39] Another flight during this time would be impossible because of a strike.

After seven weeks in Tunis, Michael, Yvonne, and Rosemarie boarded the freighter *Alfred Victory* to sail to the United States. The girls shared a bunk bed in one of the small cabins. Michael's military friend, George Carwanna, was on board and shared the cabin with them.

Stella Zampa in New York
City. Photo courtesy of the
Zampa Family.

The freighter was to dock in New York, but after fifteen days at sea they were rerouted to Boston. Once in Boston they took a train to their final destination, Detroit. Like many immigrants, they had contacts in America that would meet them and help to support them until they got their feet on the ground. This case was no different. Uncle Manuel Zampa and Aunt Josephine met them and invited them into their home on Virginia Street in Detroit.

Manuel Zampa entered the United States in 1929 on a visitor's visa. Like many of his countrymen, his plan was to earn some money and return home to open a business, in Manuel's case a clothing store. With the Depression on it was difficult to earn any significant amount of money. Manuel worked as a cook at the Book-Cadillac Hotel in Detroit. He was fired for telling a woman she "looked plenty fat to him" after the woman had stated she did not want some of the richer food because she was on a diet. According to Manuel, in Malta chubbiness due to a good diet was a sign of health. Apparently something got lost in translation. It is said that in order to feed himself through the Depression Manuel bought a tuxedo and ate uninvited at high-class weddings and parties.

After arriving in Detroit, Manuel connected with the social organizations in the Maltese community. Through these groups he met his wife, Josephine. He would have to leave America and return to Malta to renew his visa. He did so and reentered the United States and returned to Detroit and Josephine in 1936. The two were married in 1937. Josephine came to the States in April 1925 with her mother and two brothers, five years after her father came to Detroit. Josephine's family lived on West Vernon close to Tiger Stadium.

With Michael and two of the girls in the States it was time for the rest of the family to come over. Victor, Henry, Margaret, Marion, and Irene accompanied their mother, Stella, aboard the *Marine Shark* deporting from Grand Harbor in July 1947. Victor felt a bit uncomfortable aboard the ship, as some of its passengers were Italian immigrants who had recently been their enemies in the war. The family sailed for seven days on the Atlantic:

> Finally, on July 25, 1947 we passed through the Verrazano Narrows. I vividly remember the green shoreline, after being so long at sea. We sailed towards the Statue of Liberty. The lady with the torch was truly a welcome sight. Coming to a haven of liberty meant so much to us after having seen the sacrifices that must be made to defend and nurture freedom.[40]

Michael Zampa met the family at the docks on the west side of Manhattan. They all boarded the train to travel to the family flat in Detroit on Virginia Street.

Connections to the Church

The Maltese are clearly affiliated with one religious group. It is easy to understand from their history that 98 percent of Maltese adhere to the Roman Catholic faith.

The Maltese who came to America and to Michigan kept their allegiance to the Roman Catholic Church. The Catholic church of the first Maltese in Detroit was staffed by Maltese priests. Father Attard tells of the early Maltese church in Detroit:

> A prominent Maltese within the community in Detroit since 1920 was the Rev. Michael Borg who had arrived in that city to work among the Maltese in December 1920. The Maltese greeted their priest with enthusiasm. The "Detroit News" of November 13 had already received the news from Malta that a priest was going to Detroit to be put in charge of the Maltese living in that city. Under the heading: "Native Comes to Countrymen Here" the newspaper reproduced a photograph of the thirty-four-year old priest who had seen active service during the Great War and who was due to arrive shortly in New York from Cherbourg on the ship "Olympic."[41]

The Maltese in Detroit made a specific request for a Maltese-speaking priest to help reinforce the identity of the Maltese. Father Borg began his service to

LEFT: Tony Zampa poses for his First Communion along with brothers Jerry and Romeo who have just completed their confirmation. Photo courtesy of the Zampa Family.

BELOW: Maltese boys receiving awards for their work in the Maltese clubs run by the Catholic priests. Photo courtesy of the Zampa Family.

Maltese Religious and National Holidays

January 1	New Year's Day
February 10	Feast of St. Paul's Shipwreck
March 19	St. Joseph's Day
March 31	Freedom Day
May 1	Labour Day
June 7	Sette Giugno (Commemoration of 1919 Riot)
June 29	Feast of St. Peter and St. Paul
August 14	Assumption Day
September 8	Our Lady of Victories
September 21	Independence Day
December 8	Immaculate Conception
December 13	Republic Day
December 25	Christmas Day

the Maltese parishioners of Detroit by preaching in Maltese at the Knights of Equity Hall through an appointment by Bishop Michael Gallagher. The bishop himself must have welcomed the addition of a Maltese parish, as the Maltese would increase the number of Roman Catholics practicing within the diocese. Although the immediate need to retain Maltese identity through the appointment of Father Borg had been met, Bernice Stewart, of the *Detroit News,* expressed concern about the priest's ability to understand the economic situation facing the Maltese in Detroit: "He knows so little about the secular side of our industrial life that it is difficult to see how he will be able to give his parishioners the advice about material ways and means they so patently need."[42] The factors that led some of the Maltese to enter the United States (poverty and the imbalance of men over women) were still recognized as important issues to be addressed, prompting Father Borg himself in 1921 to ask a Maltese newspaper to "tell the Maltese not to come over here at the present because there are many out of work . . . next March or April will be a good time to come."[43]

Over time, the adherence and loyalty to the Roman Catholic faith along with the goal of raising funds to obtain a church structure of their own

Bishop George J. Caruana

Born: October 28, 1882, Malta

Died: March 25, 1951, Montgomery County, Pennsylvania

Father Caruana conducted missionary work in the Philippines. He spent time in Brooklyn as a parish priest. World War I saw him serve as a U.S. chaplain in the Panama Canal Zone and Puerto Rico until 1919. After the war he served as secretary to Cardinal Dougherty, archbishop of Philadelphia. He was named Bishop of the Diocese of Puerto Rico in 1921 by Pope Benedict XV. In 1927 he was appointed as Apostolic Internuncio in Haiti. His final appointment was in Cuba in 1935 as the Apostolic Nuncio.

Bishop Caruana's relationship with Father Borg and his parishioners remained strong throughout the years. Bishop Caruana's return visit to the Maltese parish in Detroit saw Father Borg present the bishop with a pectoral cross as the choirs of the Holy Trinity and Holy Rosary churches sang in unison.

began to bring the Maltese together in greater numbers. The positive effect the church and social groups were having on the image of the Maltese in the city was noted by Bernice Stewart, who wrote in a piece for the *Detroit News* that the men were now performing Shakespeare and providing musical entertainment.

The increase in Maltese attending mass during Lent of 1921 did not go unnoticed in the community. James L. Devlin of the *Detroit News* wrote, "In order to accommodate the immense number of worshippers, additional services are being held daily. Salvatore Pulis Felice erected an altar, helped by artisans many of whom are out of work. The altar is in simple Roman style and furnished in old ivory."[44] Father Borg invited two additional Maltese priests, Reverend George Caruana and Reverend James Baldacchino, to Detroit to help preside over services.

According to the *Michigan Catholic* of November 14, 1922, the Maltese were intending to collect $200,000 to achieve their wish of a permanent structure for their parish of their own design. Pledges were made payable to

Bishop Gallagher and sent to Father Borg at his residence on Baker Street or to the Maltese American Printing Company.[45]

Paul Spiteri's account of the efforts to build a new church has Father Borg taking "over an old church on 2219 Fourth Avenue and Plum Street in Detroit, which he re-named as 'Saint Paul's Maltese.'"[46] In 1927 Reverend Michael Z. Cefai of Senglea took over the responsibilities of the parish at that location, where classes in English and crafts took place as well as the formation of troops of Boy Scouts and Girl Scouts by Michael Gauci and Mary Bartolo.[47]

After the 1940s Saint Paul's Maltese and the encompassing area were at risk financially, and some accounts note concern for the physical condition of the church itself. Even though the parishioners collected $100,000 for repairs, the Detroit Catholic diocese was said to be discouraging the rehabilitation of ethnic churches, and Father Cefai was not allowed to proceed with the necessary renovations. As a result, Father Cefai was reassigned to Madonna parish at Oakland Boulevard and Twelfth Street. The name of his new church was changed to Madonna and St. Paul's in an effort to attract Maltese, but the people did not follow.[48]

The Maltese would remain loyal to the church, but the 1950s saw the development of another group, led by Joseph Calleja. Calleja organized the Malta Friendship League, which adhered to strict Catholic principles. The League used the auditorium at Holy Redeemer Catholic Church, where the group held dinners, produced Maltese plays and skits, and supported family gatherings. Calleja headed the organization until he returned to Malta. At that time John B. Abela of Valletta took over the leadership of the League.[49]

Continuing the proud tradition and strong roots of the Maltese in their Catholic faith, Father Joseph Mallia was given the honorary title of canon in the Church of the Immaculate Conception in Cospicua, Malta. Father Mallia was ordained in 1922 and was the chaplain of the Maltese American Community Club in Dearborn. Paul Borg, president of the Maltese American Community Club, in an article for the *Michigan Catholic*, reinforced the importance of Father Mallia's work with the Maltese community in maintaining important traditions for the 40,000 first- and second-generation Maltese he estimates to be in the area.

The Struggle to Become "American"

Maltese priests, acting through the National Welfare Conference, advocated for Congress to relax the 1921 and 1924 laws limiting immigration. The strong Maltese connection to the Roman Catholic Church made the Maltese attentive to the pleas of other Catholics when they encouraged the Maltese to assimilate. Americanization committees worked diligently to teach immigrants to appreciate and understand democracy.

The industrial city of Detroit had the largest Maltese colony, which by 1924 probably counted some 5,000 members. Most of the men worked in the car industry. The Americanization Committee of Detroit established a Maltese Information Bureau, which printed a circular letter in Maltese. The letter contained important information on many matters that would interest those who had just arrived in the city. The Bureau was under the direction of a Maltese immigrant, Ed Camilleri. This gentleman was active in his community, and in 1927 he was given the responsibility to help in the process of Americanizing the Maltese by giving them all the help they needed to assimilate. Camilleri wrote the circular letter, and in it he stated that the Americanisation Committee of Detroit was chiefly concerned with the process of adjusting peoples of an alien background to the requirements of the American environment.[50]

Maltese immigrants at an Americanization meeting at the home of Frank Agius,
Detroit, May 1920. Credit Line: Bentley Library, University of Michigan (YMCA of
Metropolitan Detroit records, Box 2 image bl004022).

Anne Brophy reminds us that "citywide Americanization first came to Detroit
as a response to manufacturers' fears of unrest among immigrant workers,
fears triggered by the 1914–1915 recession."[51] Detroit manufacturers were not
hiring immigrant workers because they lacked the skills necessary to work
the lines. They "were unskilled because they spoke no English and were not
American citizens."[52] This declaration saw the organization of immigrants
into social groups to support Americanization. This would shift Americanization efforts from volunteer agencies to structured public and private social
welfare groups. A November 3, 1922, *Detroit News* article reported on the
work of "Americanisers" working among the Maltese immigrants through a
group labeled the Trinity Club. The club was organized by a group of Catholic
women who focused on sponsoring social functions to better connect the
Maltese to their American Catholic counterparts. The Knights of Equity
Hall served as a gathering place where traditional American functions were
mixed in with Maltese functions to aid in assimilation.

The support given to the Maltese in Detroit was for those who had successfully emigrated. President Harding's Emergency Quota Act limited the
number of immigrants to 3 percent of those already in the country. For the
Maltese this meant few, if any, of their countrymen would be allowed legal
entry. This quota system would be even more restrictive with the 1924 act,
which limited the number of immigrants to 2 percent of the 1890 census for
any nationality. This act would not be taken lightly by the Maltese, and seri-
ous work was done to address the nationalistic attitudes expressed by the
immigration restrictions of the early 1920s.

Bishop Caruana, now in Puerto Rico and a friend of the Maltese in Detroit, took it upon himself to convey the hardships of the Maltese to the 1923
American Bishops' Conference in Washington, DC, as they related to the 1921
immigration restrictions. The bishop, born in Sliema, was able to convey his
concerns over the quotas as both a countryman and as a religious leader with
ties to the Maltese community in Detroit.

The quota system and the separation it caused among married couples
and the high poverty levels in the city were seen as the cause for the failure of
many Maltese marriages. At one point it was estimated that there were only
38 Maltese men for every 1,000 Maltese women in the United States. Hard
work on the part of several American consuls in Malta and their contacts
allowed for the sharing of "Britain's quota when that quota was not fully
used. This meant that at first some sixty Maltese were allowed to proceed to
the USA but eventually this figure was raised to ninety-six until in 1925 the
annual intake from Malta was permitted to go up to two hundred."[53]

Similar to other ethnic groups, many Maltese changed their names to
make their American transformation "complete." Father Lawrence Attard
noted that William Farr was originally William Farrugia, a watch repairer
who worked at 1385 Trubmull Avenue, Highland Park. Father Attard also
suggests that names such as Camilleri and Mizzi were changed to Miller and
Mitchell, respectively.[54]

Keeping the Maltese Identity

One way for an ethnic group to establish itself in a community was through the media. The need for immigrants to know they were in a familiar setting could help them carry the customs, folklore, language, and customs of their home country to their new world. The Maltese in Detroit established this link between their old and new identities through media and social events that helped reinforce their identity.

In the Press

The first attempt at a weekly paper for the Maltese in Detroit had its roots at the Maltese American Printing Company. This is the same company that was collecting donations for the building of a church. The paper was first published on March 10, 1922, cost five cents, and carried the name *Il Malti-American*. The paper was published in Maltese and English and served as the print voice of the Maltese American Association. The aim of the paper was to serve the Maltese immigrant population in the same way other ethnic papers in the city were doing for their communities. The main force behind *Il Malti-American* was Joseph P. Attard. Prior to Father Borg's arrival in Detroit, Attard served as the means by which the poor were fed as well as serving as the community leader for the Maltese through the Maltese Association of Detroit. The paper only lasted nine months because of low readership. It was also thought that there was a difference of opinion between Attard and Father Borg over the building of a church at the expense of the Maltese community, which Attard felt was not in a financial position to do so.[55]

Replacing *Il Malti-American* was *The Maltese Echo in America*, which began publication in 1922. The title suggests a paper that represented the culture of Malta while at the same time helping to support the Americanization of the Maltese in Detroit. This paper, too, was short-lived and ceased publication in 1924.[56]

Finally, in 1924, the *Malta Press* attempted to keep a strong ethnic voice among the Maltese in Detroit. This paper did not receive support from the community, and it too did not last beyond a few published copies.[57]

Currently, the only Maltese newspaper printed in North America is *L-Ahbar*. It is published on a monthly basis in Ontario, Canada, by Qormi Publishing. Those interested in connecting with Malta via the Web can gain easy access by linking to the *Times of Malta, maltatoday, Malta Independent,* or maltastar.com.

On the Radio

Foreign-language broadcasts in the Detroit area and the surrounding suburbs were aired by Detroit's WJLB radio. WJLB ran programming in twelve languages, including Maltese, through 1966. Father Attard recalls "two weekly radio programs in Maltese, one was prepared by the Editor of The Malta News, Mr G. Bonavia, which emanated from C.J.S.P., Leamington, Ontario, the other was the work of Mr Joseph Calleja, M.B.E., founder of the Malta Information Center, broadcasting from W.J.L.B., Detroit, Michigan."[58]

Social Events

Domus Melitensis, or Maltese House, was the name given to the basement of the Knights of Equity Hall that served the Maltese community so well in Detroit. Here is where a makeshift theater, named the Melita Dramatic Company, conducted theatrical performances. The following program advertised an April 8, 1922, performance of the company:

Dancing with family and neighbors at Harlow Street, Detroit.
Photo courtesy of the Zampa Family.

In Maltese:

Culhatt ghal basement
tad-Domus Melitensis.
Il Cumpannija Filodrammatica "Melita"
tipprezenta
It-Tebgha fil-familja.
Dramm sociali bi 3 atti.
Farsa brilliantissima.
Cuncert cbir canzonisticu.

In English:

Calling everybody to the basement
of Domus Melitensis.
The "Melita" Dramatic Company

presents

A Stain on the Family's Name. Social Play in 3 acts.

A witty comic sketch.

Song Festival.[59]

The Domus Melitensis supported several of the Maltese community's social needs, such as the Maltese Band, the Melita Athletic Club, the Maltese United Club, the Sons of Malta, the Melita Football Club, and the Detroit String Orchestra.[60]

All of these social activities were supported by the pastor of the church and were critical in developing an active Maltese presence in the city. Father Borg's hope was that the social center in this basement would grow to new bounds when connected to a new church structure.

In 1922, through the efforts to the parish, a trip was organized to Bob-Lo Island. This particular event boasted a tug-of-war and a football match. The visitors to the island were said to be made up mostly of Maltese, but Americans and Mexicans also accompanied the group.[61] Bob-Lo Island remained a popular spot for these types of social outings, with music and dancing along with amusement park rides. As the population of Maltese began to shift to the suburbs, outings and family events took place at spots like Camp Dearborn and Kensington Metropark.

Spreading the Maltese Language

For those Maltese nationals and second- and third-generation Maltese who do not live in Malta but wish to learn the language, the Maltese government has set up a program entitled *Xerred il-Malti* (Spread Maltese). It is run through the Maltese Education Ministry and is funded to support five scholarships for a course at the University of Malta.[62]

Traditional weddings, funerals, baptisms, and other events such as religious holidays rooted in the Roman Catholic faith rounded out the social gatherings the Maltese participated in to keep close the traditions and customs they held so important.

The Measure of Success

During the first wave of immigration in the 1920s some Maltese opened up their own eateries. One place at 972 Michigan Avenue was called the So Different Restaurant, boasting that it was "The best place to eat." Other eateries followed, such as the Melita Bakery at 2511 Fifth Street, which achieved popularity because it could offer breads baked in the traditional Maltese style.[63]

Father Attard writes of several other local Maltese businesses during this period. Grech and Brincat operated the General Grocers on Howard Street; John Vella ran the School of Dancing at 1355 Howard Street; and Anthony De Guara, a tailor, cleaned and pressed clothes at Sixth and Porter Streets.[64]

Most Maltese entering the States after World War II were literate and filled with hope for a better future. The Maltese had been schooled in English prior to coming to America, but now the educational system would require them to use it to gain access to the American Dream.

John R. Gatt of Mosta, Malta, arrived in America in 1920. Like many others, he worked hard and raised a family on wages obtained from work in the auto industry. Gatt worked at Ford Motor Company until retirement in 1964. He started as a machinist and achieved the position of process engineer in the Engine and Foundry Division. He married and had five children.[65]

The opportunity for his children to successfully complete high school

Marion Zampa in Silema, Malta, as a young girl. Photo courtesy of the Zampa Family.

and attend college must have been a point of pride similar to that felt by immigrants. Gatt's son, Michael, became a production control superintendent with the Ford Motor Company, while his other son, Johnny, earned a master's degree in business administration and became a career officer at the rank of major in the U.S. Air Force.

As Marion Zampa's family moved within the city of Detroit, the constant in her schooling was attendance at Catholic schools. Support from the nuns and priests at St. Theresa's, St. Scholastica's, and Benedictine, and volunteering at the Little Sisters of the Poor, laid the foundation for her eventual choice to enter the convent. In August 1958, one month shy of her sixteenth birthday, Marion entered the Dominican Motherhouse in Adrian, Michigan.

Marion's first assignment after taking her vows was to teach second grade in Escanaba, Michigan. Here she taught drama in addition to her regular assignment. Her assignment also included work on an Indian reservation and work at the Marquette Branch Prison. Marion speaks highly of the people in the Upper Peninsula and the quality of her experiences in the wild outdoors and deep snow.

After completing the architectural program at the University of Detroit with the support of scholarships and earnings from the Ford and Dodge auto plants, Victor Zampa entered the U.S. Army near the end of the Korean conflict and served with the Fourth Armored Division. After his discharge in 1955 he used the G.I. Bill to attend night school and earn an M.B.A.

In 1959 Victor joined the architectural firm of Eero Saarinen, who had immigrated to Michigan from Finland to follow in his father's fine tradition in the profession. Victor Zampa worked on projects such as Western Union Labs in Holmdel, New Jersey, IBM Labs in Yorktown, New York, the Gateway Arch, St. Louis, Lincoln Center Theater, New York, Dulles Airport, Herndon, Virginia, and the Oakland Museum, Oakland, California. In 1967, Victor worked on the Ingham Medical Center in Lansing, Michigan, which focused his work in hospital design. A departure from this specialization was his involvement in the Royal Saudi Naval Academy near Jubail.

Henry (Hank) Zampa applied to the University of Detroit Dental School after being discharged from the army. His friends were all engineers and told him that Ford Motor Company would send him to school and then hire him upon graduation. Hank quickly moved from detailer B to A, and then from designer B to A. Eventually he became a senior design engineer and took early retirement after thirty years of service with Ford Motor Company. After a failed attempt at a restaurant, Hank and his wife Carol became involved in the Amway business. Today they run an Internet-based business under the name Quixtar.com, where they work with countries all over the world.[66]

Other families with roots in Detroit, such as the Vassallo family from Marsa, Malta, saw their children achieve status in academia. Professor Paul Vassallo emigrated to America when he was fifteen. He graduated from Wayne State University and received an M.A. from the University of Michigan. He has been the head of the Washington Research Library Consortium and has held positions at the Library of Congress.[67] Still others have been technological innovators, such as John Schembri, who has two patents to his name in the area of fiber optics.[68]

Like so many other small immigrant groups, the Maltese have moved beyond the limitations of the labor as tailor, seamstress, carpenter, machinist, stonecutter, electrician, baker, mechanic, and plaster that served them well when they first arrived in their new country. While still gravitating towards these original work patterns, they have also pushed the generations of Maltese-Americans that came after them into the roles of teacher, clergy, CEO, doctor, scientist, small business owner, actor, and musician, to name a few.

This little-known group, the Maltese, has indeed left its mark as one of the peoples of Michigan.

Appendix 1

Maltese Food

The Maltese are renowned for their good humor and cheer. One immigrant, Irene (Zampa) Lubig recalled that this humor and cheer is clearly evident around the family gatherings.

> We would always have dinner together and when we were finished we would stay at the dinner table and have fun telling stories and teasing each other. One time we laughed so hard I remember Yvonne falling off her chair backwards. Henry's and Vic's friends, Bob and Jake, would come over and tell us stories and tease Mom. She would laugh and have a good time with them. She loved all the attention they gave her and they enjoyed her company. They would bring her chocolates sometimes because they knew she really liked them. Those were really fun times. I wish we had those days back.

Many Maltese had excellent recipes for rabbit stew, baked leg of lamb, or roasts. Fish of all kinds was popular, with fish heads considered a delicacy in some families. Due to the lack of firewood ovens in centuries past, a slow cooking method was used to prepare most Maltese dishes. Food was placed in earthenware pots over a little stone hearth called a kenur, which needed constant tending and fanning. Subsequently, slow simmering became

something of the hallmark of many Maltese dishes and despite the intro-
duction of gas and electric cookers, slow cooking is still a favorite method
(Scicluna 1999).

Fried Rabbit (Fenek Moqli)

rabbit
oil
fresh garlic
dry white wine
thyme
salt and pepper

Cut the rabbit into medium-sized pieces. Chop the garlic. In a large bowl
place the rabbit and cover with white wine. Mix in the garlic and thyme with
some salt and pepper. Cover and leave in the fridge overnight or for a minimum of six hours.

In a large shallow frying pan heat the oil. Add the garlic to the oil when
hot and fry for a few minutes over medium heat. Insert the rabbit pieces into
the pan and fry. Turn the pieces occasionally and cook well. Sprinkle with dry
white wine while cooking and add salt and pepper to taste.

Spaghetti with Octopus Sauce: *Spaghetti Biz-Zalza Tal-Qarnit* (Stella Zampa)

2 lbs. octopus or squid
8 oz. onions
6 oz. peas
8 oz. tomatoes
4 oz. black olives
1 cup red wine
1½ lbs. spaghetti
3 oz. tomato paste
herbs
mint
lemon zest

olive oil

salt and pepper to taste

Peel and slice the onions. Cut the octopus into even-sized pieces and fry in
a little oil and water. Add the tomato paste and herbs and continue cooking
for about 15 minutes. Prepare the tomato sauce by peeling the tomatoes and
chopping them finely. Strain the octopus but save the liquid. Slice the olives.
Add the onions, tomatoes, olives, red wine, tomato paste, herbs, mint, and
lemon zest. Simmer for 15 minutes. Add the octopus liquid and simmer for
another 15 minutes. Serve over spaghetti noodles.

Baked Macaroni: *Imquarrun Fil-Forn* (Stella Zampa)

TOMATO SAUCE:

1 can tomato sauce or diced canned tomatoes

4 oz. onions

2 lbs. bacon or ground beef

1 cup water

bay leaf

olive oil

garlic clove

salt and ground pepper

Finely chop the onions and garlic. Heat the olive oil and sauté the onion and
garlic. Add the meat and cook until golden brown. Add the tomato sauce or
diced tomatoes, tomato paste, and water. Bring to a boil and add bay leaf,
salt, and pepper. Simmer for 45 minutes.

1½ lbs. long macaroni noodles

½ tsp. garlic powder or fresh garlic cloves

6 eggs lightly beaten

¼ cup grated Parmesan cheese

1 lb. ricotta can be added if the cook wishes

Cook the large macaroni, drain, and rinse. Slightly beat the eggs and add to
the macaroni and gently stir in the cheese.

After the tomato sauce is done simmering, add it to the pasta and gently stir. Pour the mixture into a lightly greased deep baking dish. Beat two more eggs and pour them on top of the macaroni dish along with more grated cheese. Bake at 375° for one hour or until the top is brown and crisp.

Stuffed Eggplant: *Bringiel Mimli* (Zampa family)

1 large eggplant
1 lb. of ground beef
1 medium onion chopped
1 egg slightly beaten
1 Tbs. tomato paste
1 tsp. grated cheese
dash of allspice
dash of marjoram
salt and pepper to taste

Cut the eggplant in half lengthwise. Place in a pot of water and boil for about 15 minutes. Remove the eggplant from the water. Spoon out the center and chop the center into small pieces.

In a large bowl combine the beef, onion, egg, tomato paste, eggplant center, cheese, and spices. Mix well. Fill the eggplant halves evenly with the meat mixture. Place the stuffed eggplant in a roasting pan. Add a little water and bake for 1½ hours at 350°. Whole carrots and onions may be put into the roasting pan and cooked along with the eggplant for a complete dinner.

Fried Eggplant: *Bringiel Moqli* (Zampa family)

1 large eggplant
½ cup flour
¼ tsp. garlic salt
salt and pepper
olive oil for frying

Cut eggplant into small, round, thin slices. In a paper bag combine the flour, garlic salt, and pepper. Put the eggplant sliced in the bag and shake until the eggplant is covered with the flour mixture. Fry in hot oil until brown. Serve hot or cold. A tomato wine sauce with capers can be used to top off this dish if served cold.

Stuffed Artichokes (Irene Lubig)

4 artichokes

FILLING:

4 slices of bread cubed
½ cup chopped olives
½ cup capers
½ cup chopped parsley
2 cloves chopped garlic
1 can of chopped anchovies (optional)
salt and pepper
1 Tbs. olive oil
1 Tbs. vinegar

Rinse artichokes. To make the filling, mix the bread, olives, capers, parsley, garlic, salt, pepper, anchovies, oil, and vinegar. Mix well.

Stand artichokes. Fill with mixture between leaves and in the center. Place the artichokes in a deep pot. Fill the pot half way with water. Add salt to the water and bring to a boil. Cover and let simmer for one hour or until the leaves come off easily. Serve hot or cold.

To eat the artichoke, pull the leaves out one at a time. Pull the filling and meat off with your teeth and enjoy. If you are not familiar with artichokes, be careful when you get to the heart, which is the last part in the center. The leaves may seem a little prickly so just pull the tops off and eat around them.

Stuffed Zucchini: *Qara' Baghli Mimili Bil-Laham* (Zampa family)

4 large zucchini
1 lb. minced meat or ground beef
3 oz. onions
2 oz. grated cheese
2 eggs

1 oz. tomato paste
1½ lbs. potatos
chopped parsley
clove of garlic
salt and pepper
olive oil

Cut the zucchini tops and scoop out the pulp. Chop the onions and garlic and fry in the hot oil, being careful not to brown them. Add the tomato paste and the meat. Continue cooking until the meat is completely cooked. Add the chopped pulp and continue cooking. Allow this mixture to cool. Slightly beat and add the eggs, cheese, parsley, and seasonings. Fill the zucchini and place them on a bed of sliced potato. Bake for 1 to 1½ hours at 350°.

Fried Zucchini: *Qara' Moqli* (Margaret Laybourn)

medium-sized zucchini
canola oil
olive oil
onions diced
garlic clove
tomato paste
tomato sauce
water equal to a can of tomato sauce or a bit more
capers
salad olives diced
black olives diced

Before frying the zucchini wash and cut into circle pieces, not too thin. Place in a colander to drain the excess juices and lightly salt. Heat the canola oil in a skillet (olive oil burns and loses its flavor when used for long frying time). Fry each slice of zucchini, placing the fried slices in a colander to drain the excess oil.

SAUCE: Sauté the onion and garlic, adding the tomato products and water. Simmer gently. Add the capers. Be sure to include 1 tsp. of caper vinegar, chopped black olives, salad olives. Continue to simmer for 15 minutes. Cool the mixture. Place the fried zucchini in a bowl and pour the mixture over the zucchini. Serve hot or cold.

Pastizzi (Rosemarie Camilleri)

3 cups of shortening
5 cups of flour
2 cups of cold water
dash of salt
Ricotta filling:
1 lb. ricotta
1 egg
1 Tbs. grated Parmesan cheese
salt and pepper

Put the flour, water, and salt in a bowl and mix with an electric mixer with dough hook or in a large bowl by hand. Mix the same as you would for bread, about 20 minutes. The dough should feel slightly moist and soft as a baby's behind. Cover with a light layer of shortening and refrigerate overnight. Cut off about ⅛ of the dough and stretch it out like pizza dough on a slightly greased counter. Pull and spread in all directions a little at a time until the dough is very thin. Spread a generous amount of shortening over the top of the dough. Start at one end of the dough and roll, being sure to pull back and up on the dough as you roll. Repeat this process adding each layer until the roll is about 1½ inches thick. Cover and refrigerate until ready for use.

When ready to roll out, cut the dough roll into 1½-inch sections. Lay each piece on its side so the circles are facing up. Spread each circle out carefully. Put approximately one tablespoon of the filling mix in the middle of each circle. Fold both sides over the filling and press each end down. Bake 1 hour at 375°. Cook until lightly browned.

A Eulogy for Mary Stella and Michael L. Zampa Delivered by Victor M. Zampa, 12 August 1987

The eulogy here was delivered by Victor M. Zampa, the eldest son of Mary Stella and Michael L. Zampa, at their funeral on August 12, 1987, at St. Genevieve's Church in Livonia, Michigan. It has been included as an appendix because the pride and joy reflected in their history is one similar to many immigrants and their families. It reflects on the struggles and triumphs common to those who sought a better life in America.

As we bid this temporary farewell to my parents, I would like to share with you a few thoughts about their lives. Some of you have known them in their later years, when time had perhaps already started to take its toll—in ways that were sometimes subtle, sometimes cruel. But, as their eldest son, I've had the pleasure and the privilege of knowing them as a young couple.

They had their virtues and their human weaknesses, as you and I; their joys and their sorrows; their days of turmoil and days of peace. They were very much in love with each other, and as such they knew hurt, and they knew forgiveness. And there were qualities about them that were distinctively their own.

My mother had an innate love of beauty. She loved beauty in her personal possessions, in her adornments and her clothes; and she loved beauty in her home and her garden—and she worked constantly at this. She also very much loved the beauty of making music in the choir at St. Genevieve's. I know she held that very close to her heart from the way she talked about it; that was certainly one of the highlights of her life. She also was very appreciative of our accomplishments, whether large or small, or even trivial. Both she and Dad were very proud of our successes, and they let us know it.

Yet I think one of the qualities that I really will remember best is their limitless capacity for self-sacrifice, especially when it came to the family. My mother raised seven children while my dad was in the military. Much of the time she had to be a single parent—and this was during World War II, on an island which was being bombed several times a day for a number of years. And that must have been very difficult. My dad, on his part, had to endure many forced separations from his family, including during wartime, and he had to do his best to keep our spirits and keep food on the table. And I must say to their credit that we never felt insecure; we always felt very much protected in the comforts of the family, no matter what was happening around us. And we hardly ever felt hungry either—at least, not really hungry anyway.

My dad's military career started in the United States when he came here as a young man. He joined the United States Marines and was stationed in Quantico, Virginia, and at Guantánamo. He went back to Malta for what he thought would be a short trip; however, he met my mother and in 1929 they were married. That was in January of 1929—he was twenty-five, she was twenty years old.

Of course, family ties being strong back there, he stayed in Malta. He joined the British navy and stayed there throughout the thirties. In the forties he served in the British army through the world war, and in 1946 he came back to the United States—we'd always talked about doing that. He came back with two of my sisters. My mother and I and the rest of my sisters and my brother followed in 1947.

This life of his was quite rigorous, and I would think my mother's life always seemed to be full of hard work. However, we had some very wonderful moments together, and I can remember when he was in the navy and he was about to come home. My mother would run around the house and do a little bit more dusting, polishing and straightening up than usual—and I know my sisters will find this very hard to believe, but she did—and she wanted to make sure that she was ready to welcome her sailor home from the sea. And then we'd go to the shoreline and wave the ship in. He'd come to shore; there'd be hugs and kisses and tears of joy, and then for a number of days we had just a tremendous time as a family. We'd go to the beach together, on the blue Mediterranean; we'd go to restaurants and theatres, and we'd have picnics and visit relatives; and on Sunday we'd walk down the street to church together, dressed in our Sunday best.

Those were wonderful times and through it all there was one thing that really struck us—especially me, I think I could say, because I was the oldest—really struck us about my father: and that was how much he cared for and loved my mother. And that's really strange because, in those days, in that generation, there really wasn't much outward show of affection between parents. Everybody was somewhat staid and formal and all that sort of stuff. But you could see it; you could see it in their little actions, in the way they would talk to each other, and even in the way they walked together. I feel that his devotion to her was so uncompromising, so profound and so committed, that I just wonder if she herself even fully understood it. And I really don't think he even fully understood it to tell you the truth.

But one of the hardest things for me while they were in the hospital and were sick, lately, was to see how little they could really do for each other. They really wanted to help each other and they would ask about each other; and they'd be home at the same time or at the hospital at the same time but they were so near and yet so far. Just a few weeks ago, I remember putting my mother in a wheelchair at the hospital and taking her to see my dad. And he was already in pain, but when he saw her so helpless—and she really couldn't talk and could hardly move—there was a deeper pain in his eyes, but only for a moment. Then he just brightened up and smiled and he said, "Stella, we just have to stop meeting like this," and that made me feel a little better. He really didn't think that anybody else could take care of her the way he did and, well, he was probably right. He waited her out. He just wanted to make sure she was safely in the arms of the Lord before he left, and he was. And true to her own style, she did go ahead of him up there about a day or so. And I'm sure when she went up to Heaven she must've looked around and made sure that everything was really ship-shape and straightened out and in good order; because she wanted to welcome her sailor, home from the storm.

Now, in the words of Thomas Moore, I do believe that "Earth has no sorrow that heaven cannot heal," and they must be enjoying a truly perfect union up there for all eternity. However, I've had a wish I'd like to share with you. I wish that perhaps the Lord will let some little flaw or some slight imperfection creep into His Kingdom; it wouldn't take very much—just enough for my mother to say, "Mike, there's something I'd like you to fix for me up here." And you know, his eyes would light up, and that broad, warm smile would come across his face, and he would say to himself, "She needs me. She still needs me."

Well, we're not closing the book on my parents today; we're just turning over a page. A part of them will always be a part of us and our children. Please pray for them and pray for them with joy and music, the way my mother would love to hear it; and if it pleases her, I'm sure my father would be very happy. Thank you.

Appendix 3

Maltese Surnames

The Maltese are a difficult group to identify and study, as they are often labeled as immigrants from Europe or the British Commonwealth. To discover a history of the Maltese, researchers have had to rely on the registries of the Catholic churches in Detroit and Maltese clubs and societies formed in the Detroit area (Maltese-American Benevolent Society; Sons and Daughters of St. Paul). Joseph H. Muscat, a Maltese, conducting research for a master's thesis at Wayne State University in the early 1970s, resorted to scanning the telephone directories of Detroit and its suburbs to compile a list of surnames from which to obtain a survey sample for his research. When completed, his list showed a total of 1,700 names recognizable as Maltese, with 900 found in the city of Detroit and the remaining 800 in the suburbs. Some of the surnames noted where those of the following families:

Abdilla	Azzopardi	Borg
Abela	Bartolo	Brincat
Agius	Bezzina	Bugeja
Aquilina	Bonavia	Buhagiar
Attard	Bonnello	Busuttil
Axiak	Bonnici	Buttigieg

Cachia	Fava	Saliba
Calleja	Fenech	Sammut
Camilleri	Fiteni	Sant
Carabott	Formosa	Sapiano
Caruana	Frendo	Scerri
Casha	Galea	Schembri
Cassar	Gatt	Sciberras
Cauchi	Gauci	Scicluna
Cefai	Grech	Scriha
Chetcuti	Grima	Spiteri
Chircop	Hili	Sultana
Ciantar	Mallia	Tabone
Cini	Meli	Tanti
Curmi	Mercieca	Testa
Cuschieri	Micallef	Theuma
Cutajar	Mifsud	Tonna
Dalli	Mizzi	Vassallo
Darmanin	Muscat	Vella
Debono	Naudi	Xuereb
Desira	Pace	Zahra
Dimech	Pisani	Zammit
Ebejer	Portelli	Zarb
Ellul	Psaila	Zerafa
Falzon	Pulis	
Farrugia	Said	

Appendix 4

Language

Bilingualism was often necessary in the workplace and the written language, until mid-1860, was never Maltese. Prior to 1934, Italian was used in the workplace, taught in the schools, and was the official language of the courts until replaced with English.

The Maltese language is derived from the Arab dialect spoken during the early Middle Ages. The language has strong Italian and English influences. It is the only Semitic language written in the Latin alphabet. Maltese and English are the official languages of Malta.

There are some variations in the sounds of letters. For speakers of American English to pronounce Maltese, they need to recognize the following sounds of letters:

- [ċ] is pronounced like our "ch."
- [h] is silent within a word and pronounced like our "h" when at the end of a word.
- [j] is pronounced like our "y."
- [gh] is mostly silent but prolongs the sound of a vowel when it proceeds the vowel; when [gh] is at the end of a word, it is pronounced as a soft "h."

- [q] used in a way similar to our (') in words to denote sudden separation of sounds.
- [r] is trilled like the Scottish "r."
- [x] is pronounced like our "sh."
- [ż] is pronounced like our "z."
- [z] is pronounced like our "ts."

Basic Words and Common Expressions in Maltese

ENGLISH	MALTESE	PRONUNCIATION
Simple words		
Yes	Iva	iva
No	Le	le
Please	Jekk joghbok	yek yo : jbok
Thank you	Grazzi	gratsi
You're welcome	M'hemmx mn'hiex	memsh mni : sh
Greetings		
How are you?	Kif inti?	kiyf inti
Very well, thanks. And you? (*male*)		
	Tajjeb hafna. U inti?	tayeb hafna u inti
Very well, thanks. And you? (*female*)		
	Tajba hafna. U inti?	tayba hafna u inti
Good morning	Bongu	bonju
Good evening	Bonswa	bonswa
Good-bye	Sahha	sahha
I beg your pardon?	Skuzi?	skuzi
Excuse me!	Skuzi!	skuzi
Sorry	Skuzani	skuza : ni
Questions		
Do you speak English?	Titkellem bl-Ingliz?	titkellem bl ingli : s
Can you tell me?	Tista' tghidli?	tista teydli
Can you help me?	Tista' tghinni?	tista teyni
Can I help you?	Nista' nghinek?	nista neyneyk
How much?	Kemm?	kem
How long?	Kemm iddum?	kem iddu : m

The oldest known literary text in the Maltese language, "Il Cantilena," dates to the fifteenth century and is credited to Pietru Caxaro. The text in Maltese with an English translation follows. The poem is said to speak through metaphor of a failed romance.

Xideu il cada ye gireni tale nichadithicum
Mensab fil gueri uele nisab fo homorcom
Calb mehandihe chakim soltan ui le mule
Bir imgamic rimitne betiragin mucsule
Fen hayran al garca nenzel fi tirag minzeli
Nitla vu nargia ninzil deyem fil bachar il hali.

Huakit hi mirammiti lili zimen nibni
Mectatilix mihallimin me chitali tafal morchi
fen timayt insib il gebel sib tafal morchi
vackit hi mirammiti.

Huakit by mirammiti Nizlit hi li sisen
Mectatilix li mihallimin ma kitatili li gebel
fen tumayt insib il gebel sib tafal morchi
Huakit thi mirammiti lili zimen nibni
Huec ucakit hi mirammiti vargia ibnie
biddilihe inte il miken illi yeutihe
Min ibidill il miken ibidil i vintura
haliex liradi 'al col xibir sura
hemme ard bayad v hemme ard seude et hamyra
Hactar min hedann heme tred mine tamara.

———

Witness my predicament, my friends (neighbors), as I shall relate it to you:
Never has there been, neither in the past, nor in your lifetime,
A [similar] heart, ungoverned, without lord or king (sultan),
That threw me down a well, with broken stairs
Where, yearning to drown, I descend the steps of my downfall,

Climb back up, only to go down again in this sea of woe.

It (she) fell, my edifice, [that] which I had been building for so long,
It was not the builders' fault, but (of) the soft clay (that lay beneath);
Where I had hoped to find rock, I found loose clay.
It (she) fell, my building!

It (she) fell, my building, its foundations collapsed;
It was not the builders' fault, but the rock gave way,
Where I had hoped to find rock, I found loose clay
It (she) fell, my edifice, (that) which I had been building for so long,
And so, my edifice subsided, and I shall have to build it up again,
Change the site that caused its downfall.
Who changes his place, changes his "vintura"!
For each (piece of land) has its own shape (features);
There is white land and there is black land, and red.
But above all, you must stay clear of it.

2000 Census of Maltese in Michigan

The following information denotes the Maltese population in Michigan according to the 2000 census.

CITY	COUNTY	MALTESE POPULATION
St. Joseph Charter	Berrien	6
Battle Creek	Calhoun	6
Delta Charter	Eaton	6
Waverly	Eaton	6
Davison	Genesee	10
Fenton	Genesee	20
Fenton Township	Genesee	38
Flint	Genesee	6
Flint Township	Genesee	65
Flushing	Genesee	9
Grand Blanc	Genesee	32
Mundy	Genesee	17
Traverse City	Grand Traverse	3
East Lansing	Ingham	47
Lansing	Ingham	23
Meridian Charter	Ingham	15

CITY	COUNTY	MALTESE POPULATION
Okemos	Ingham	15
Mount Pleasant	Isabella	14
Leoni	Jackson	17
Comstock	Kalamazoo	7
Kalamazoo	Kalamazoo	21
Oshtemo	Kalamazoo	8
Portage	Kalamazoo	4
Allendale	Kent	17
East Grand Rapids	Kent	12
Forest Hills	Kent	8
Grand Rapids	Kent	27
Kentwood	Kent	32
Walker	Kent	15
Brighton	Livingston	92
Genoa Township	Livingston	38
Green Oak	Livingston	45
Hamburg	Livingston	96
Hartland	Livingston	40
Chesterfield	Macomb	72
Clinton	Macomb	210
Eastpointe	Macomb	24
Fraser	Macomb	28
Harrison	Macomb	60
Macomb Township	Macomb	207
Roseville	Macomb	103
St. Clair Shores	Macomb	151
Shelby	Macomb	162
Sterling Heights	Macomb	418
Warren	Macomb	258
Washington Township	Macomb	71
Marquette	Marquette	5
Big Rapids	Mecosta	6
Midland	Midland	6
Bedford	Monroe	11
Fruitport Charter	Muskegon	4

CITY	COUNTY	MALTESE POPULATION
Norton Shores	Muskegon	3
Auburn Hills	Oakland	24
Berkely	Oakland	40
Birmingham	Oakland	67
Bloomfield	Oakland	70
Brandon	Oakland	15
Clawson	Oakland	53
Commerce	Oakland	230
Farmington	Oakland	46
Farmington Hills	Oakland	145
Ferndale	Oakland	35
Hazel Park	Oakland	108
Highland	Oakland	80
Independence	Oakland	24
Lyon	Oakland	13
Madison Heights	Oakland	15
Milford	Oakland	144
Mount Clemens	Oakland	24
Novi	Oakland	171
Orion	Oakland	118
Oxford Charter	Oakland	50
Pontiac	Oakland	9
Rochester	Oakland	53
Rochester Hills	Oakland	129
Royal Oak	Oakland	166
South Lyon	Oakland	100
Southfield	Oakland	38
Southfield Township	Oakland	16
Springfield	Oakland	46
Troy	Oakland	104
Waterford	Oakland	50
West Bloomfield	Oakland	115
White Lake	Oakland	170
Wixom	Oakland	159
Georgetown	Ottawa	5

CITY	COUNTY	MALTESE POPULATION
Jenison	Ottawa	5
Saginaw Charter	Saginaw	27
Saginaw Township North	Saginaw	27
Port Huron	Saint Clair	6
Owosso	Shiawassee	9
Ann Arbor	Washtenaw	55
Pittsfield Charter	Washtenaw	6
Scio	Washtenaw	10
Ypsilanti	Washtenaw	14
Ypsilanti Township	Washtenaw	18
Allen Park	Wayne	265
Brownstone	Wayne	100
Canton	Wayne	592
Dearborn	Wayne	626
Dearborn Heights	Wayne	656
Detroit	Wayne	473
Ecorse	Wayne	7
Garden City	Wayne	211
Grosse Ile	Wayne	131
Grosse Pointe Park	Wayne	5
Grosse Pointe Woods	Wayne	36
Hamtramck	Wayne	8
Harper Woods	Wayne	31
Huron Charter	Wayne	27
Inkster	Wayne	53
Lincoln Park	Wayne	110
Livonia	Wayne	942
Melvindale	Wayne	26
Northville	Wayne	89
Plymouth Township	Wayne	108
Redford	Wayne	251
Riverview	Wayne	77
Romulus	Wayne	19
Southgate	Wayne	184
Sumpter	Wayne	5

CITY	COUNTY	MALTESE POPULATION
Taylor	Wayne	296
Trenton	Wayne	103
Van Buren Township	Wayne	55
Wayne	Wayne	71
Westland	Wayne	519
Woodhaven	Wayne	123
Wyandotte	Wayne	111
TOTAL		11,735

Reflections on World War II

Victor Zampa. Born March 3, 1931, Valletta, Malta

On a September day in 1939, Mom's [Stella Zampa's] brother Manwel burst into our home and announced, "The war has started. The Germans have invaded Poland." This abruptly changed our lives. Earlier that year, Mom had become very worried about Dad's safety while at sea. One evening, after one of his trips, when my siblings were with some nearby relatives, my mom's feelings came to a head and I stood helplessly by as she tearfully implored dad to leave the navy. This meant he would have to give up a career he had thrived on and forfeit time that would have counted towards a retirement pension. She painted him a grim picture of his becoming lost at sea. She won the argument; he left the HMS *Grenville* and, on December 4, 1939, Dad joined the King's Own Malta Regiment and was stationed in Malta. On January 19, 1940, the *Grenville* hit a German mine and sank in the North Sea. I still have the February 2 issue of *The War Illustrated* showing a front-page photograph of the destroyer's bow about to slip under the waves with a lone sailor balancing himself on a porthole. That particular sailor was saved; many of Dad's friends weren't.

Watching aerial dogfights became something of a spectator sport during the raids. At the start of the war we had only three Gladiator biplanes (nicknamed *Faith, Hope,* and *Charity*) to confront squadrons of Italian bombers which were soon to be accompanied by fighter escorts. They gave a very good account of themselves against superior forces and *Faith* still survives as an exhibit among Malta's war memorabilia. Later on we acquired Hurricanes, which had a difficult time against the faster Messerschmitt fighters and Stuka dive bombers. Finally, Spitfires arrived to level out the playing field. It certainly was exciting to watch the tactics of their planes and ours, often culminating in the losers ditching their craft and parachuting down to be met on the ground by whoever got there first. I never heard of any enemy airmen being mistreated after capture. I only got to see them behind their POW compound fences. Once, while some friends and I were hiking in the countryside, we came upon a compound for German prisoners. Some of them tried to communicate with us, but language problems prevented a meaningful exchange. Then one of them saw me admiring a carved limestone ashtray he was holding, slipped it through the fence and gave it to me. We both smiled and I thanked him, wondering, as we walked away, how all this fit in with bitter enmities and mortal combat.

We were strengthened by Churchill's inspiring oratory, the spirit of the Great Siege of 1565, and a deep pervasive faith—to such intangibles we owed our continuing freedom and, most likely, our lives. Later, more material help started to arrive in the form of better fighter planes, more trained pilots, and supply convoys that made it through, many of them badly battered—an indication of what their crews had to endure on their desperate journey. One could hear a collective sigh of relief when the United States entered the war in December 1941. Life had become quite a contrast to the prewar days. Food vendors no longer plied the streets and had been replaced by communal cooking stations called "victory kitchens." We would line up for a bowl of stew containing, among other things, the latest raid kills—horse and goat meat were often nonfeatured highlights of the menu. Fortunately, the central bakeries common to most neighborhoods on the island remained in business; they would take in raw prepared dishes from customers and, for a fee, bake them in high-heat ovens, resulting in very tasty dishes made from any available ingredients—far better than could be produced on the kerosene cooking equipment common to most homes. Dad's farmer friends would also bring him fresh fruit and vegetables once in a while.

I remember one day when a tanker in one of the harbors was hit and thick black smoke spewed high into the sky. After the raid, mom took us all for a walk along the waterfront—Maggie, Hank, Yvonne, Rosemarie, little Marion, and myself. All the girls were wearing beautiful sweaters and skirts she had knitted for them. Suddenly, the cloud of smoke from the burning oil started to condense, and black droplets came down like a fine mist, completely ruining my sisters' clothes. All Mom could do was hustle us back home, but only after the damage had been done. The damage to the island's oil supplies was the real concern, however. It was in August 1942, with fuel, food, and ammunition stores at their low point of the war years, that what was left of a tenacious convoy, symbolized by the heavily damaged American tanker the SS *Ohio*, arrived with desperately needed provisions. That proved to be a turning point in the struggle, paving the way to adopting an increasingly aggressive stance against enemy supplies headed for our esteemed adversary Field Marshal Rommel in North Africa and, when the Afrika Korps capitulated in mid-May 1943, preventing Rommel's remaining troops from escaping by sea. The frequency of enemy raids started to subside, and in June 1943 King George VI paid us a surprise visit. I remember standing along the waterfront in Sliema and waving enthusiastically as he went by in an open convertible in a rapidly moving motorcade.

Margaret (Zampa) Laybourn. Born March 1, 1932, Valletta, Malta

We had to stay out of Valletta because of the bombing, so Dad got us to the country areas until he could find a place for us. He found a house to rent closer to his base in Busket. Guiza and Nanna Karmena and Nannu Vincent went together to another house and Dad's parents went to Birkirkara. Nannu Paul owned a grocery store at that time and his dad's sister Paula lived there.

Dad finally finished moving our whole family to Sliema near Auntie Netta. He had planned on doing this before the war had started. When we finally got moved into Sliema, we helped Netta and her husband Joseph and all the neighbors finish building the bomb shelter. Everyone had to help dig out the shelters. We all did it with shovels and buckets. It is still there.

When air raids started, Ma had a bed in the kitchen part and she would stay there so she would be ready to take us to the shelter. She was pregnant with Marion, and during one of the air raids she delivered Marion in the kitchen and then went down to shelter right after. I had to run down the street to get the midwife. I was always the one to run out and get the midwife.

The shelter wasn't that far away from our house; we would grab our blankets and go down there. The air raids were terrible, but the noise, the sound of women praying the rosary, the crying and smells made being in the shelter a nightmare.

I used to have to go and get the bottles of milk at five o'clock in the morning. I would stand in line at the milk depot for a bottle of milk. Dad wasn't home, so Ma couldn't go. Whenever I had to get the milk, she told me that if the bombs started to fall, go into the first shelter I saw. One time an air raid started and I was almost home and I was afraid to go into a shelter by myself without any of my family there. So I kept dodging the bombs by going from door to door to protect myself. A German airplane came down low, shooting a machine gun down the street. I got hit on the back of my legs because I was facing the door. The house was Auntie Annie's house. It had double doors and an arch over the door. The ground shook from all the bombings and I dropped the bottle and started crying, not because I got hit but because I broke the bottle of milk. I was bleeding, but it didn't bother me as much as breaking the damn bottle of milk.

A bomb hit my girlfriend's house and killed her whole family. The bomb came down while I was in the street. It was like a torpedo going over the houses. I was twelve years old at the time and had to help Mom with everything. The shelters always had to have two openings, but when the bomb hit, one of the shelter openings became blocked. People who ended up with no housing had to find shelter with other families. Most of our food was canned food. I used to love the caramelized canned milk. We would walk over the rubble to get food from the military. Vic wasn't around a lot because he was always involved with the Salesians. I used to help Ma with the kids. When the war was slowing down and the war was almost over, the ships started to come into port. Some ships were from Turkey, so the Maltese people would hide the girls because they were afraid they would be kidnapped. I don't think that was true—people were still fearful from past wars and occupations in Malta.

Henry Zampa. Born August 20, 1933, Valletta, Malta

I hated to go down to the shelters. Vic also put up a fuss when it was time to go down there. I would sneak out and look at the planes in dogfights or watch the rockets go off. It looked like fireworks. It was very colorful to watch, especially at night. This is how I got some of the scars on my body. One night I was out looking at the planes. I could hear the bombs coming down, and I could tell they were close and I did not have much time to get to the bomb shelter. We would figure out how much time we had by the sound of the planes or loudness of the bombs. One came down and the explosion threw me against the house and cut me up in different places. I was bleeding like crazy. Ma saw me coming down the stairs and she screamed and then I got scared because I knew I would probably get in lots of trouble. When she saw that I was okay she started hitting me, "Pow, pow, pow." She was so mad at me for scaring her that she scared me even more than the bombs. Every time we had to go to the bomb shelter, Ma would always call, "Henry. Henry! Where is Henry?" She wanted to make sure I went down with everyone.

Dad was stationed in Malta during the war. He had been reassigned from the NAAFI to the King's Own Malta Regiment. Vic and I would sometimes spend time with Dad at his base playing soldiers. I still have his swagger stick and bayonet. When we visited there we would see the German soldiers who were prisoners. We would pass chocolate candy through the barbed wire to them. Dad was a quartermaster and sometimes he would send a truck over to us with food. Ma would store some under our steps and in the shelter.

I enjoyed the Salesian priests because they got us involved in a lot of different things. Our favorite priests were Father DiGeorgio and Father Borg. Vic and I were in the boys' brigade, where we learned military style marching and parading. Most of my high school years were spent with them. We used to play soccer a lot on the playgrounds. I learned to play the clarinet and I was in the marching band for the fiestas. That was the biggest part of our lives. We also attended the lyceum government school. We took a lot of courses: Italian, Latin, French, and Maltese. We had to take buses to the schools. Then we would go to the Salesian Oratory after that. Schooling and Salesian programs continued throughout the war. I remember running home from there and a German plane was shooting a machine gun right down the street. I still remember hearing the "ppppppp" sound of the gun. They attacked us a lot. When the Americans came through from the African shores, the attacks started to slow down.

Yvonne (Zampa) Burns. Born November 9, 1934, Valletta, Malta

The air raids and the bomb shelter is still a memory for me. I would hear the sirens and we would have to run down to the underground bomb shelter. We spent many nights there; we even had our own little room with cots for sleeping. There seemed to be a lot of old ladies dressed in black crying while saying the rosary over and over again. That sound is still hard to get out of my mind. That is probably why I didn't like it when we would have to say the rosary after dinner time. One time we slept in our house during an air raid because we were all so tired from running into the shelter. When we woke up we saw a German airplane that had come down in flames. Ma would always be there to help people that were hurt. I don't know how she managed all of us during the war.

Much of our food was imported, but before the ships would reach port, most of the time they were bombed. We lived on cans of sardines a lot. Food was rationed during the war and we had to stand in line to get our share of food and milk. We mostly grew up on powdered milk during the war. Malta was heavily bombed but we fought back and survived; at the time we were under the British rule.

Rosemarie (Zampa) Camilleri. Born October 8, 1937, Valletta, Malta

When the war started I was three years old. Ma had so many relatives and they spent lots of time talking to each other but not the kids. I used to enjoy Nanna and Nannu Bugeja coming to visit and going to Nanna and Nannu Zampa's candy store. They used to give us a piece of candy when we went there.

During the war I remember trying to get out of the back door on Hyacinth Street and running down into the shelter with Auntie Netta's family. I remember running into the shelter and Ma would be calling and looking for Vic and Hank. Sometimes they stayed asleep because they didn't want to get up and go down into the shelter. She would have to go back and wake them up and make them come down. We ate lots of sardines and anchovies because we couldn't get enough food to feed the people during the war. We drank canned milk and sometimes we had fresh milk. When people died in Malta they laid them out in their house. I remember a lady across the street died and we went over there. I would get really scared whenever we had to do this. I would just back away from the body.

Marion (Glass) Zampa. Born September 6, 1941, Sliema, Malta

The war in Malta was very difficult for its people. By April 1942 Malta had experienced her darkest hours. Ten thousand buildings had been destroyed. Germany and Italy flew at least 400 sorties a day. The schools stayed open so the children could be occupied with more than the war. During the air raids they would be sent to the shelters near their homes or stay in the school shelters. As a toddler I remember the darkness and mostly crying. To this day I still dread the dark. The old women in black would be sitting on cots moaning and chanting the rosary. The Maltese people are a very religious nationality. They prayed the rosary to the Virgin Mary to protect the island. I have a few images of walking across the rubble towards the end of the war, going with my sisters to get a cup of milk in my white porcelain mug. We ate lots of sardines and anchovies (which I still love) and other canned food, because Germany set up blockades to starve the Maltese people in order to force them to surrender. Several attempts made by sea to resupply Malta were attacked by German planes. Germany calculated if the island people were starved, then they would surrender and Germany would have a hold on the Mediterranean. The British-manned *Ohio*, an American-made vessel, was the first one to reach Malta's Grand Harbor in the cover of dark. People gathered at the Grand Harbor to cheer the ship into port. The cargo was unloaded amid air strikes. The Germans failed to break the spirit and bravery of the Maltese people. This is the same strength that carried my parents and siblings through those challenging years and all the years to come. In June 1943 King George VI awarded the entire population of Malta the George Cross for their bravery. This award had never been given to all the citizens of a country before. He visited Malta with his daughter Elizabeth (Queen Elizabeth II) to present the award.

Appendix 7

Maltese Ethnic and Social Organizations

- American-Maltese Community Club of Dearborn, 5221 Oakman Blvd., Dearborn, MI 48126; (313) 846-7077
- Consulate General of Malta, The Honorable Larry J. Zahra, Honorary Consul General, 26953 Sheahan Dr., Dearborn Heights, MI 48127; (313) 563-1779
- Maltese-American Benevolent Society, 1832 Michigan Avenue, Detroit, MI 48216; (313) 310-9121
- Most Holy Trinity Rectory, 1050 Porter Street, Detroit, MI 48226; (313) 965-4450
- Maltese American Social Club of San Francisco, 924 El Camino Real, South San Francisco, CA 94080; (650) 871-4611
- The Maltese Center of Astoria, New York, Malta Square, 27-20 Hoyt Avenue, South Astoria, NY 11102-1942; (718) 728-9883

Maltese-Related Websites

- Independent website addressing Maltese migration and maintained on a voluntary basis: www.maltamigration.com
- Maltese-American Student Association, University of Michigan–Dearborn, www.facebook.com

- Malta United Society of Windsor, Ontario, Canada, http://www.maltawindsor.com/
- A link to Maltese media abroad: http://www.aboutmalta.com/grazio/mediabroad.html

Notes

1. See the website detailing statistics on Malta at http://geography.about.com/library/cia/blcmalta.htm. Accessed on 12 September 2008.

2. Information on Popeye Village Fun Park, http://www.popeyemalta.com. Accessed on 8 September 2008.

3. Judith M. Calleja, "Factors Enhancing the Rapid Assimilation of Maltese Immigrants in Detroit," *Central Issues in Anthropology: A Journal of the Central States Anthropological Society* 6 (1985): 1–10.

4. Colin Renfrew, *Before Civilization* (London: Pimlico, 1973), 147.

5. Ibid.

6. Ibid.

7. James Stafford, *Malta* (Bromall, PA: Mason Crest Publishers, 2006).

8. William S. Ellis, "Malta: The Passion and Freedom," *National Geographic*, June 1989, 700–717.

9. Ibid., 708.

10. Ibid.

11. See online resource outlining key events in Malta's history, http://www.about-malta.com. Accessed on 17 July 2007.

12. Ibid.

13. United States of America Embassy in Malta webpage, http://malta.usembassy.gov/new_embassy_in_malta_project.html, provides an image of "The Bells First

Note" by Jean Leon Gerome Ferris (1863–1930).

14. Diane Andreassi, "Maltese American Highlights," http://www.everyculture. com/multi/Le-Pa/Maltese-Americans.html. Accessed on 5 January 2009.

15. *Maltese International* is an independent bimonthly newspaper published for Maltese living abroad.

16. "Chamber Hosts Distinguished U.S. Visitors," *Maltese International* 5, no. 1 (January 1990): 6.

17. Andreassi, "Maltese American Highlights."

18. James Anderson and Iva Smith, eds., *Ethnic Groups in Michigan* (Ann Arbor: University of Michigan Press, 1983).

19. Ibid.

20. Taken from a collected family history of the Mike and Stella Zampa family.

21. J. H. Muscat, "Some Characteristics of the Maltese People in Metropolitan Detroit." Master's thesis, School of Social Work, Wayne State University, 1974.

22. P. Spiteri, "History of the Maltese Immigrants in the State of Michigan, U.S.A.," manuscript in the State Library of Michigan, 1970, 4.

23. Ibid.

24. Ibid.

25. Ibid.

26. Bernice Stewart, "Maltese Colony Is Largest in America," *Detroit Free Press*, 12 December 1920, 3.

27. Stephan Thernstrom, ed., *Harvard Encyclopedia of American Ethnic Groups* (Cambridge: Harvard University Press, 1980), 695.

28. Ibid.

29. Central Office of Statistics Malta, "Demographic Review of the Maltese Islands for the Year 1968," 45.

30. Anderson and Smith, *Ethnic Groups in Michigan*.

31. Geoff Dench, *Maltese in London: A Case-Study in the Erosion of Ethnic Consciousness* (London: Routledge and Kegan Paul, 1975).

32. Calleja, "Factors Enhancing Assimilation," 2–3.

33. Sidney Glazer, *Detroit: A Study in Urban Development* (New York: Bookman Associates, 1965).

34. Calleja, "Factors Enhancing Assimilation."

35. Ibid.

36. Phone interview with Irene Lubig, 7 November 2005.

37. Calleja, "Factors Enhancing Assimilation."

38. Mary M. Kalergis, *Home of the Brave: Contemporary American Immigrants* (New York: E. P. Dutton, 1989).

39. Personal communication with Rosemarie Camilleri.

40. Personal communication with Victor Zampa.

41. Information found at www.maltamigration.com. Accessed on 6 January 2009.

42. Lawrence E. Attard, *Man and Means: Early Maltese Emigration, 1900–1914* (Gulf Publications, 1983).

43. Ibid.

44. James L. Devlin, *Detroit News*, 20 March 1921.

45. Lawrence E. Attard, *The Great Exodus*, http://www.maltamigration.com/history/exodus/. Accessed on 15 August 2007.

46. Spiteri, "History of Maltese Immigrants," 6.

47. Ibid., 6–7.

48. Ibid., 16.

49. Ibid., 20.

50. Information found at www.maltamigration.com. Accessed on 6 January 2009.

51. Anne Brophy, "'The Committee . . . Has Stood Out against Coercion': The Reinvention of Detroit Americanization, 1915–1931," *Michigan Historical Review* 29 (2003): 9.

52. Ibid.

53. Attard, *The Great Exodus*.

54. Ibid.

55. Ibid.

56. Ibid.

57. Ibid.

58. Ibid.

59. Ibid.

60. Ibid.

61. Ibid.

62. "Spreading Maltese Among Non-Resident Nationals," www.timesofmalta.com, 3 August 2010. Specific link to article found at http://www.timesofmalta.com/articles/view/20100803/local/spreading-maltese-through-education-among-non-resident-nationals. Accessed on 7 August 2010.

63. Attard, *The Great Exodus*.

64. Ibid.

65. Spiteri, "History of Maltese Immigrants" 13.

66. Taken from a collected family history of the Mike and Stella Zampa family.

67. Andreassi, "Maltese American Highlights."

68. Ibid.

For Further Reference

Archives and Libraries

Archdiocese of Detroit, Detroit, MI 48226; (313) 224-8000; FAX (313) 224-8009. Resource: *The Michigan Catholic* newspaper, available online in searchable format: http://www.aodonline.org/AODOnline/News+++Publications+2203/Michigan+Catholic+News+12203/2010+17545/July.htm.

Bentley Historical Library, University of Michigan, 1150 Beal Ave., Ann Arbor, MI 48109-3482; (734) 764-3482; FAX (734) 936-1333; http://bentley.umich.edu/.

Published Sources

Attard, Lawrence E. *Early Maltese Emigration: 1900–1914.* Valletta: Gulf, 1983.

———. *The Safety Valve: A history of Maltese Emigration from 1946.* Malta: PEG, 1997.

Austin, Dennis. *Malta and the End of Empire.* London: Frank Cass, 1971.

Balm, Roger. *Malta.* Blacksburg, VA: McDonald & Woodard, 1995.

Blouet, Brian. *A Short History of Malta.* New York: Frederick Praeger, 1967.

Blouet, Brian. *The Story of Malta.* Malta: Progress Press, 1989.

Boissevain, Jeremy. *Saints and Fireworks: Religion and Politics in Rural Malta.* London: Athlone Press, 1965.

———. *A Village in Malta.* New York: Holt, Rinehart & Winston, 1980.

Casolani, H. *Awake Malta.* Malta, 1930.

Cassar, Paul. *Early Relations between Malta and USA*. Malta: Midsea Books, 1976.

Dobie, Edith. *Malta's Road to Independence*. Norman: University of Oklahoma Press, 1967.

The Epic of Malta: A Pictorial Survey of Malta during the Second World War. Odhams Press, 1943.

Evans, J. D. *The Prehistoric Antiquities of the Maltese Islands: A Survey*. London: Athlone Press, 1971.

Luke, Harry. *Malta: An Account and an Appreciation*. 2nd ed. London: G. G. Harrap, 1968.

The Malta Yearbook. Sliema, Malta: De La Salle Brothers, 1991.

Muscat, Joseph H. "Some Characteristics of the Maltese People in Metropolitan Detroit." Master's thesis, School of Social Work, Wayne State University, 1974.

Price, Charles A. *Malta and the Maltese: A Study in Nineteenth Century Migration*. Melbourne, Australia, 1954.

Scicluna, Frank. "Legends, Customs, and Beliefs." 1999. http://www.allmalta.com/folklore/customs.html. Accessed on 10 March 2009.

Trump, D. H. *Malta: An Archeological Guide*. London: Faber and Faber, 1972.

Woodford, Frank B., and Arthur M. Woodford. *All of Our Yesterdays: A Brief History of Detroit*. Wayne State University Press, 1969.

Online Resources

Maltese migration with a strong emphasis on the United States and Australia: www.maltamigration.com.

This day in history site for Malta: http://www.maltesering.com/today.asp.

Tourism site for the country of Malta: http://www.visitmalta.com/main?1=1.

University of Malta: http://www.um.edu.mt/.

World War II photo index of Malta: http://www.killifish.f9.co.uk/Malta%20WWII/Index.htm.

Index